CHRISTMAS

ITS ORIGIN, CELEBRATION AND SIGNIFICANCE AS RELATED IN PROSE AND VERSE

Robert Haven Schauffler

CONTENTS

NOTE

PREFACE

INTRODUCTION

I

ORIGIN

3

II
CELEBRATION

Sly Santa Claus	*Mrs. C.S. Stone*
The Waits	*Margaret Deland*
The Knighting of the Sirloin	*Anonymous*
The Christmas Goose at the Cratchits'	*Charles Dickens*
God Bless Us Every One	*James Whitcomb Riley*
Bells Across the Snow	*Frances Ridley Havergal*
Christmas Bells	*Henry Wadsworth Longfellow*
Minstrels and Maids	*William Morris*
Inexhaustibility of the Subject of Christmas	*Leigh Hunt*
Song of the Holly	*William Shakespeare*
Under the Holly-Bough	*Charles Mackay*
Ceremonies for Christmas	*Robert Herrick*
Santa Claus	*Anonymous*
The Ceremonies for Christmas Day	*Robert Herrick*
December	*Harriet F. Blodgett*
The Festival of St. Nicholas	*Mary Mapes Dodge*
The Christmas Holly	*Eliza Cook*
To the Fir-Tree	*From the German*
The Mahogany-Tree	*William Makepeace Thackeray*
Christmas	*Washington Irving*
Church Decking at Christmas	*William Wordsworth*
So, Now is Come Our Joyful'st Feast	*George Wither*

IV
STORIES

V
OLD CAROLS AND EXERCISES

God Rest You, Merry Gentlemen

PREFACE

Christmas is our most important holiday, and its literature is correspondingly rich. Yet until now no adequate bundle of Christmas treasures in poetry and prose has found its way into the library of Santa Claus.

While this book brings to children of all ages, in school and at home, the best lyrics, carols, essays, plays and stories of Christmas, its scope is yet wider. For the Introduction gives a rapid view of the holiday's origin and development, its relation to cognate pagan festivals, the customs and symbols of its observance in different lands, and the significance and spirit of the day. This Introduction endeavors to be as suggestive as possible to parents and teachers who are personally conducted and introduced to the host of writers learned and quaint, human and pedantic, humorous and brilliant and profound, who have dealt technically with this fascinating subject.

INTRODUCTION

It was the habit of him whose birthday we celebrate to take what was good in men and remould it to higher uses. And so it is peculiarly fitting that the anniversary of Christmas, when it was first celebrated in the second century of our era should have taken from heathen mythology and customs the more beautiful parts for its own use. "Christmas," says Dean Stanley, "brings before us the relations of the Christian religion to the religions which went before; for the birth at Bethlehem was itself a link with the past."

The pagan nations of antiquity[A] always had a tendency to worship the sun, under different names, as the giver of light and life. And their festivals in its honor took place near the winter solstice, the shortest day in the year, when the sun in December begins its upward course, thrilling men with the first distant promise of spring. This holiday was called *Saturnalia* among the Romans and was marked by great merriment and licence which extended even to the slaves. There were feasting and gifts and the houses were hung with evergreens. A more barbarous form of these rejoicings took place among the rude peoples of the north where great blocks of wood blazed in honor of Odin and Thor, and sacrifices of men and cattle were made to them.

Mistletoe was cut then from the sacred oaks with a golden sickle by the Prince of the Druids, between whom and the Fire-Worshippers of Persia there was an affinity both in character and customs.

[A]An account of the early history of Christmas may be found in Chamber's Book of Days.

The ancient Goths and Saxons called this festival Yule, which is preserved to us in the Scottish word for Christmas and also in the name of the Yule Log. The ancient Teutons celebrated the season by decking a fir tree, for they thought of the sun, riding higher and higher in the heavens, as the spreading and blossoming of a great tree. Thus our own Christmas fir was decked as a symbol of the celestial sun tree. The lights, according to Professor Schwartz, represent the flashes of lightning overhead, the golden apples, nuts and balls symbolize the sun, the moon and the stars, while the little animals hung in the branches betoken sacrifices made in gratitude to the sun god.[B]

[B]A delightful account of the origin of the Christmas tree may be found in Elise Traut's Christmas in Heart and Home.

As Christianity replaced paganism, the Christians, in the tolerant spirit of their Master, adopted these beautiful old usages, merely changing their spirit. So that the Lord of Misrule who long presided over the Christmas games of Christian England was the direct descendant of the ruler who was appointed, with considerable prerogatives, to preside over the sports of the Saturnalia. In this connection the narrow Puritan author of the "Histrio-Mastix" laments: "If we compare our Bacchanalian Christmasses with these Saturnalia, we shall find such a near affinitye between them, both in regard to time and in manner of solemnizing, that we must needs conclude the one to be but the very issue of the other."

"Merrie old England," writes Walsh,[C] "was the soil in which Merrie Christmas took its firmest root." Even in Anglo-Saxon days we hear of Alfred holding high revelry in December, 878, so that he allowed the Danes to surprise him, cut his army to pieces and send him a fugitive. The court revelries increased in splendor after the conquest. Christmas, it must be remembered was not then a single day of sport. It had the preliminary novena which began December 16, and it ended on January 6, or Twelfth Night. All this period was devoted to holiday making.

[C]Curiosities of Popular Customs.

It was a democratic festival. All classes mixed in its merry-makings. Hospitality was universal. An English country gentleman of the fifteenth and sixteenth centuries held open house. With daybreak on Christmas morning the tenants and neighbors thronged into the hall. The ale was broached. Blackjacks and Cheshire cheese, with toast and sugar and nutmeg, went plentifully round. The Hackin, or great sausage, must be boiled at daybreak, and if it failed to be ready two young men took the cook by the arm and ran her around the market-place till she was ashamed of her laziness.

With the rise of Puritanism the very existence of Christmas was threatened. Even the harmless good cheer of that season was looked upon as pagan, or, what was worse, Popish. 'Into what a stupendous *height* of more than pagan impiety,' cried Prynne (...) 'have we not now *degenerated!* Prynne's rhetoric, it will be seen, is not without an unconscious charm of humor. He complained that the England of his day could not celebrate Christmas or any other festival 'without drinking, roaring, healthing, dicing, carding, dancing, masques and stage-plays (...) which Turkes and Infidels would abhor to practise.'

Puritanism brought over with it in the Mayflower the anti-Christmas feeling to New England. So early as 1621 Governor Bradford was called upon to administer a rebuke to 'certain lusty yonge men' who had just come over in the little ship Fortune. 'On ye day called Christmas day,' says William Bradford, 'ye Govr caled them out to worke (as was used), but ye most of this new company excused themselves and said it went against their consciences to worke on ye day. So ye Govr tould them that if they made it matter of conscience, he would spare them till they were better informed. So he led away ye rest, and left them; but when they came home at noone from their worke, he found them in ye streete at play, openly: some pitching ye barr, and some at stoole-ball and such like sports. So he went to them and tooke away their implements, and tould them that it was against his conscience that they should play and others worke. If they made ye keeping of it matter of devotion, let them kepe their houses, but ther should be no gameing or revelling in ye streets. Since which time nothing hath been attempted that way, at least openly.'

In England the feeling culminated in 1643, when the Roundhead Parliament abolished the observance of saints' days and "the three grand festivals" of Christmas, Easter, and Whitsuntide, "any law, statute, custom, constitution, or canon to the contrary in any wise notwithstanding." The king protested. But he was answered. In London, nevertheless, there was an alarming disposition to observe Christmas. The mob attacked those who by opening their shops flouted the holiday. In several counties the disorder was threatening. But Parliament adopted strong measures, and during the twelve years in which the great festivals were discountenanced there was no further tumult, and the observance of Christmas as a general holiday ceased. The General Court of Massachusetts followed the example of the English Parliament in 1659 when it enacted that 'anybody who is found observing, by abstinence from labor, feasting, or any other way, any such day as Christmas day, shall pay for every such offense five shillings.'

The restoration of English royalty brought about the restoration of the English Christmas. It was not till 1681, however, that Massachusetts repealed the ordinance of 1659. But the repeal was bitter to old Puritanism, which kept up an ever attenuating protest even down to the early part of the present century.

There are many superstitions connected with the coming of Christmas itself. The bees are said to sing, the cattle to kneel, in honor of the manger, and the sheep to go in procession in commemoration of the visit of the angel to the shepherds. Howison in his "Sketches of Upper Canada" relates that on one moonlit Christmas Eve he saw an Indian creeping cautiously through the woods. In response to an inquiry, he said. 'Me watch to see deer kneel. Christmas night all deer kneel and look up to Great Spirit.'

In the German Alps it is believed that the cattle have the gift of language on Christmas Eve. But it is a sin to attempt to play the eavesdropper upon them. An Alpine story is told of a farmer's servant who did not believe that the cattle could speak, and, to make sure, he hid in his master's stable on Christmas Eve and listened. When the clock struck twelve he was surprised at what he heard. 'We shall have hard work to do this day week,' said one horse. 'Yes; the farmer's servant is heavy,' answered the other horse. 'And the way to the churchyard is long and steep,' said the first. The servant was buried that day week.

There is a beautiful superstition about the cock that Shakespeare put into the mouth of Marcellus, in *Hamlet*—

"Some say, that ever 'gainst that season comes
Wherein our Saviour's birth is celebrated,
The bird of dawning singeth all night long:
And then, they say, no spirit can walk abroad;
The nights are wholesome; then no planets strike,
No fairy takes, nor witch hath power to charm;
So hallow'd and so gracious is the time."

No other holiday has so rich an heritage of old customs and observances as Christmas. The Yule Log has from time immemorial been haled to the open fire-place on Christmas Eve, and lighted with the embers of its predecessor to sanctify the roof-tree and protect it against those evil spirits over whom the season is in everyway a triumph. Then the wassail bowl full of swimming roasted apples, goes its merry round. Then the gift-shadowing Christmas tree sheds its divine brilliance down the path of the coming year; or stockings are hung for Santa Claus (St. Nicholas) to fill during the night. Then the mistletoe becomes a precarious shelter for maids, and the Waits— descendants of the minstrels of old—go through the snow from door to door, singing their mellow old carols, while masquerades and the merry Christmas game of Snapdragon are not forgotten.[D]

[D]An exhaustive study of the history and customs of Christmas has been made by W.F. Dawson in "Christmas and its Associations."

Even the Christmas dinner has its special observances. In many an English hall the stately custom still survives of bearing in a boar's head to inaugurate the meal, as a reminder of the student of Queens College, Oxford, who, attacked by a boar on Christmas day, choked him with a copy of Aristotle and took his head back for dinner. The mince pie, sacred to the occasion, is supposed to commemorate in its mixture of oriental ingredients

14

the offerings made by the wise men of the East. As for turkey and plum pudding, they have a deep significance, but it is clearer to the palate than to the brain.

Elise Traut relates the legend that on every Christmas eve the little Christ-child wanders all over the world bearing on its shoulders a bundle of evergreens. Through city streets and country lanes, up and down hill, to proudest castle and lowliest hovel, through cold and storm and sleet and ice, this holy child travels, to be welcomed or rejected at the doors at which he pleads for succor. Those who would invite him and long for his coming set a lighted candle in the window to guide him on his way hither. They also believe that he comes to them in the guise of any alms-craving, wandering person who knocks humbly at their doors for sustenance, thus testing their benevolence. In many places the aid rendered the beggar is looked upon as hospitality shown to Christ.

This legend embodies the true Christmas spirit which realizes, with a rush of love to the heart, the divinity in every one of "the least of these" our brethren. Selfishness is rebuked, the feeling of universal brotherhood is fostered, while the length of this holiday season by encouraging the reunion of families and of friends, provides a wonderful rallying place for early affections. A wholesome and joyous current of religious feeling flows through the entire season to temper its extravagance and regulate its mirth.

"Under the sanctions of religion," writes Hervey,[E] "the covenants of the heart are renewed.... The lovers of Earth seem to have met together."

[E]For a beautiful and extended discussion of the significance of the day, see Hervey's "The Book of Christmas."

Christmas is the birthday of one whose chief contribution to the human heart and mind was his message of boundless, universal love, He brought to the world the greatest thing in the world and that is why the season of his birth has won such an intimate place in our hearts and why its jubilant bells find this echo there:

"Ring out the old, ring in the new,
Ring, happy bells, across the snow;
The year is going, let him go;
Ring out the false, ring in the true.

"Ring out the grief that saps the mind,
For those that here we see no more;
Ring out the feud of rich and poor,
Ring in redress to all mankind.

"Ring out a slowly dying cause,
And ancient forms of party strife;
Ring in the nobler modes of life,
With sweeter manners, purer laws.

"Ring out the want, the care, the sin,
The faithless coldness of the times;
Ring out, ring out my mournful rhymes,
But ring the fuller minstrel in.

"Ring out false pride in place and blood,
The civic slander and the spite;
Ring in the love of truth and right,
Ring in the common love of good.

"Ring out old shapes of foul disease;
Ring out the narrowing lust of gold;
Ring out the thousand wars of old,
Ring in the thousand years of peace.

"Ring in the valiant man and free,
The larger heart, the kindlier hand;
Ring out the darkness of the land,
Ring in the Christ that is to be."

R.H.S.

I

ORIGIN

IS THERE A SANTA CLAUS?

The following, reprinted from the editorial page of the New York Sun, was written by the late Mr. Frank P. Church:
We take pleasure in answering at once and thus prominently the communication below, expressing at the same time our great gratification that its faithful author is numbered among the friends of *The Sun*:
Dear Editor: I am 8 years old.
Some of my little friends say there is no Santa Claus.
Papa says "If you see it in *The Sun* it's so."
Please tell me the truth; is there a Santa Claus?
Virginia O'Hanlon.
Virginia, your little friends are wrong. They have been affected by the scepticism of a sceptical age. They do not believe except they see. They think that nothing can be which is not comprehensible by their little minds. All minds, Virginia, whether they be men's or children's, are little. In this great universe of ours man is a mere insect, an ant, in his intellect, as compared with the boundless world about him, as measured by the intelligence capable of grasping the whole of truth and knowledge.
Yes, Virginia, there is a Santa Claus. He exists as certainly as love and generosity and devotion exist, and you know that they abound and give to your life its highest beauty and joy. Alas! how dreary would be the world if there were no Santa Claus! It would be as dreary as if there were no Virginias. There would be no childlike faith then, no poetry, no romance to make tolerable this existence. We should have no enjoyment, except in sense and sight. The eternal light with which childhood fills the world would be extinguished.

Not believe in Santa Claus! You might as well not believe in fairies! You might get your papa to hire men to watch in all the chimneys on Christmas Eve to catch Santa Claus, but even if they did not see Santa Claus coming down, what would that prove? Nobody sees Santa Claus, but that is no sign that there is no Santa Claus. The most real things in the world are those that neither children nor men can see. Did you ever see fairies dancing on the lawn? Of course not, but that's no proof that they are not there. Nobody can conceive or imagine all the wonders there are unseen and unseeable in the world.

You may tear apart the baby's rattle and see what makes the noise inside, but there is a veil covering the unseen world which not the strongest man, nor even the united strength of all the strongest men that ever lived, could tear apart. Only faith, fancy, poetry, love, romance, can push aside that curtain and view and picture the supernal beauty and glory beyond. Is it all real? Ah, Virginia, in all this world there is nothing else real and abiding.

No Santa Claus! Thank God! he lives, and he lives forever. A thousand years from now, Virginia, nay, ten times ten thousand years from now, he will continue to make glad the heart of childhood.

O LITTLE TOWN OF BETHLEHEM
PHILLIPS BROOKS

O little town of Bethlehem,
How still we see thee lie!
Above thy deep and dreamless sleep
The silent stars go by;
Yet in thy dark streets shineth
The everlasting Light;
The hopes and fears of all the years
Are met in thee to-night.

For Christ is born of Mary,
And, gathered all above,
While mortals sleep, the angels keep
Their watch of wondering love.
O morning stars, together
Proclaim the holy birth!
And praises sing to God the King,
And peace to men on earth.
How silently, how silently,
The wondrous gift is given!
So God imparts to human hearts
The blessings of His heaven.
No ear may hear His coming,
But in this world of sin,
Where meek souls will receive Him still,
The dear Christ enters in.

O holy Child of Bethlehem!
Descend to us, we pray;
Cast out our sin, and enter in,
Be born in us to-day.
We hear the Christmas angels
The great glad tidings tell;
Oh, come to us, abide with us,
Our Lord Emmanuel!

THE GLAD EVANGEL
KATE DOUGLAS WIGGIN

When the Child of Nazareth was born, the sun, according to the Bosnian legend, "leaped in the heavens, and the stars around it danced. A peace came over mountain and forest. Even the rotten stump stood straight and healthy on the green hill-side. The grass was beflowered with open blossoms, incense sweet as myrrh pervaded upland and forest, birds sang on the mountain top, and all gave thanks to the great God."

It is naught but an old folk-tale, but it has truth hidden at its heart, for a strange, subtle force, a spirit of genial good-will, a new-born kindness, seem to animate child and man alike when the world pays its tribute to the "heaven-sent youngling," as the poet Drummond calls the infant Christ.

When the Three Wise Men rode from the East into the West on that "first, best Christmas night," they bore on their saddle-bows three caskets filled with gold and frankincense and myrrh, to be laid at the feet of the manger-cradled babe of Bethlehem.

Beginning with this old, old journey, the spirit of giving crept into the world's heart. As the Magi came bearing gifts, so do we also; gifts that relieve want, gifts that are sweet and fragrant with friendship, gifts that breathe love, gifts that mean service, gifts inspired still by the star that shone over the City of David nearly two thousand years ago.

Then hang the green coronet of the Christmas-tree with glittering baubles and jewels of flame; heap offerings on its emerald branches; bring the Yule log to the firing; deck the house with holly and mistletoe,

"And all the bells on earth shall ring
On Christmas day in the morning."

THE SHEPHERDS
WILLIAM DRUMMOND, OF HAWTHORNDEN

O than the fairest day, thrice fairer night!
Night to blest days in which a sun doth rise
Of which that golden eye which clears the skies
Is but a sparkling ray, a shadow-light!
And blessed ye, in silly pastor's sight,
Mild creatures, in whose warm crib now lies
That heaven-sent youngling, holy-maid-born wight,
Midst, end, beginning of our prophecies!

Blest cottage that hath flowers in winter spread,
Though withered—blessed grass that hath the grace
To deck and be a carpet to that place!
Thus sang, unto the sounds of oaten reed,
Before the Babe, the shepherds bowed on knees;
And springs ran nectar, honey dropped from trees.

A CHRISTMAS CAROL
JAMES RUSSELL LOWELL

"What means this glory round our feet,"
The Magi mused, "more bright than morn?"
And voices chanted clear and sweet,
"To-day the Prince of Peace is born!"

"What means that star," the Shepherds said,
"That brightens through the rocky glen?"
And angels, answering overhead,
Sang, "Peace on earth, good-will to men!"

'Tis eighteen hundred years and more
Since those sweet oracles were dumb;
We wait for Him, like them of yore;
Alas, He seems so slow to come!

But it was said, in words of gold,
No time or sorrow e'er shall dim,
That little children might be bold
In perfect trust to come to Him.

All round about our feet shall shine
A light like that the wise men saw,
If we our loving wills incline
To that sweet Life which is the Law.

So shall we learn to understand
The simple faith of shepherds then,
And, clasping kindly hand in hand,
Sing, "Peace on earth, good-will to men!"

But they who do their souls no wrong,
But keep at eve the faith of morn,

Shall daily hear the angel-song,
"To-day the Prince of Peace is born!"

A CHRISTMAS HYMN
ALFRED DOMETT

It was the calm and silent night!
Seven hundred years and fifty-three
Had Rome been growing up to might,
And now was Queen of land and sea.
No sound was heard of clashing wars;
Peace brooded o'er the hush'd domain;
Apollo, Pallas, Jove and Mars,
Held undisturb'd their ancient reign,
In the solemn midnight
Centuries ago.

'T was in the calm and silent night!
The senator of haughty Rome
Impatient urged his chariot's flight,
From lordly revel rolling home.
Triumphal arches gleaming swell
His breast with thoughts of boundless sway;
What reck'd the Roman what befell
A paltry province far away,
In the solemn midnight
Centuries ago!

Within that province far away
Went plodding home a weary boor:
A streak of light before him lay,
Fall'n through a half-shut stable door
Across his path. He pass'd—for nought
Told what was going on within;
How keen the stars! his only thought;
The air how calm and cold and thin,
In the solemn midnight
Centuries ago!

O strange indifference!—low and high
Drows'd over common joys and cares:
The earth was still—but knew not why;
The world was listening—unawares.
How calm a moment may precede
One that shall thrill the world for ever!
To that still moment none would heed,
Man's doom was link'd, no more to sever,
In the solemn midnight
Centuries ago.

It *is* the calm and solemn night
A thousand bells ring out, and throw
Their joyous peals abroad, and smite
The darkness, charm'd and holy now.
The night that erst no name had worn,
To it a happy name is given;
For in that stable lay new-born
The peaceful Prince of Earth and Heaven,
In the solemn midnight
Centuries ago.

BRIGHTEST AND BEST OF THE SONS OF THE MORNING
REGINALD HEBER
Brightest and best of the Sons of the morning!
Dawn on our darkness and lend us thine aid!
Star of the East, the horizon adorning,
Guide where our Infant Redeemer is laid!

Cold on His cradle the dewdrops are shining,
Low lies His head with the beasts of the stall;
Angels adore Him in slumber reclining,
Maker and Monarch and Saviour of all!

Say, shall we yield Him, in costly devotion,

Odors of Edom and offerings divine?
Gems of the mountain and pearls of the ocean,
Myrrh from the forest, or gold from the mine?

Vainly we offer each ample oblation;
Vainly with gifts would His favor secure:
Richer by far is the heart's adoration;
Dearer to God are the prayers of the poor.

Brightest and best of the Sons of the morning!
Dawn on our darkness and lend us thine aid!
Star of the East, the horizon adorning,
Guide where our Infant Redeemer is laid!

GOD REST YE, MERRY GENTLEMEN
DINAH MARIA MULOCK

God rest ye, merry gentlemen; let nothing you dismay,
For Jesus Christ, our Saviour, was born on Christmas-day.
The dawn rose red o'er Bethlehem, the stars shone through the
gray,
When Jesus Christ, our Saviour, was born on Christmas-day.

God rest ye, little children; let nothing you affright,
For Jesus Christ, your Saviour, was born this happy night;
Along the hills of Galilee the white flocks sleeping lay,
When Christ, the child of Nazareth, was born on Christmas-day.

God rest ye, all good Christians; upon this blessed morn
The Lord of all good Christians was of a woman born:
Now all your sorrows He doth heal, your sins He takes away;
For Jesus Christ, our Saviour, was born on Christmas-day.

THE CHRISTMAS SILENCE
MARGARET DELAND

Hushed are the pigeons cooing low
On dusty rafters of the loft;
And mild-eyed oxen, breathing soft,
Sleep on the fragrant hay below.

Dim shadows in the corner hide;
The glimmering lantern's rays are shed
Where one young lamb just lifts his head,
Then huddles 'gainst his mother's side.

Strange silence tingles in the air;
Through the half-open door a bar
Of light from one low-hanging star
Touches a baby's radiant hair.

No sound: the mother, kneeling, lays
Her cheek against the little face.
Oh human love! Oh heavenly grace!
'Tis yet in silence that she prays!

Ages of silence end to-night;
Then to the long-expectant earth
Glad angels come to greet His birth
In burst of music, love, and light!

A CHRISTMAS LULLABY
JOHN ADDINGTON SYMONDS

Sleep, baby, sleep! The Mother sings:
Heaven's angels kneel and fold their wings.
Sleep, baby, sleep!

With swathes of scented hay Thy bed
By Mary's hand at eve was spread.
Sleep, baby, sleep!

At midnight came the shepherds, they
Whom seraphs wakened by the way.
Sleep, baby, sleep!

And three kings from the East afar,
Ere dawn came, guided by the star.
Sleep, baby, sleep!

They brought Thee gifts of gold and gems,
Pure orient pearls, rich diadems.
Sleep, baby, sleep!

Thou who liest slumbering there,
Art King of Kings, earth, ocean, air.
Sleep, baby, sleep!

Sleep, baby, sleep! The shepherds sing:
Through heaven, through earth, hosannas ring.
Sleep, baby, sleep!

HYMN FOR THE NATIVITY
EDWARD THRING

Happy night and happy silence downward softly stealing,
Softly stealing over land and sea,
Stars from golden censors swing a silent eager feeling
Down on Judah, down on Galilee;
And all the wistful air, and earth, and sky,
Listened, listened for the gladness of a cry.

Holy night, a sudden flash of light its way is winging:
Angels, angels, all above, around;
Hark, the angel voices, hark, the angel voices singing;
And the sheep are lying on the ground.
Lo, all the wistful air, and earth, and sky,
Listen, listen to the gladness of the cry.

Happy night at Bethlehem; soft little hands are feeling,
Feeling in the manger with the kine:
Little hands, and eyelids closed in sleep, while angels kneeling,
Mary mother, hymn the Babe Divine.
Lo, all the wistful air, and earth, and sky,
Listen, listen to the gladness of the cry.

Wide, as if the light were music, flashes adoration:
"Glory be to God, nor ever cease,"
All the silence thrills, and speeds the message of salvation:
"Peace on earth, good-will to men of peace."
Lo, all the wistful air, and earth, and sky,
Listen, listen to the gladness of the cry.

Holy night, thy solemn silence evermore enfoldeth
Angels songs and peace from God on high:
Holy night, thy watcher still with faithful eye beholdeth
Wings that wave, and angel glory nigh,

Lo, hushed is strife in air, and earth, and sky,
Still thy watchers hear the gladness of the cry.

Praise Him, ye who watch the night, the silent night of ages:
Praise Him, shepherds, praise the Holy Child;
Praise Him, ye who hear the light, O praise Him, all ye sages;
Praise Him, children, praise Him meek and mild.
Lo, peace on Earth, glory to God on high,
Listen, listen to the gladness of the cry.

MASTERS IN THIS HALL
ANONYMOUS

"To Bethlem did they go, the shepherds three;
To Bethlem did they go to see whe'r it were so or no,
Whether Christ were born or no
To set men free."

Masters, in this hall,
Hear ye news to-day
Brought over sea,
And ever I you pray.

Nowell! Nowell! Nowell! Nowell!
Sing we clear!
Holpen are all folk on earth,
Born is God's Son so dear

Going over the hills,
Through the milk-white snow,
Heard I ewes bleat
While the wind did blow.
Nowell, &c.

Shepherds many an one
Sat among the sheep;
No man spake more word
Than they had been asleep.
Nowell, &c.

Quoth I 'Fellows mine,
Why this guise sit ye?
Making but dull cheer,
Shepherds though ye be?
Nowell, &c.

'Shepherds should of right
Leap and dance and sing;
Thus to see ye sit
Is a right strange thing.'
Nowell, &c.

Quoth these fellows then
'To Bethlem town we go,
To see a Mighty Lord
Lie in manger low.'
Nowell, &c.

'How name ye this Lord,
Shepherds?' then said I.
'Very God' they said,
'Come from Heaven high.'
Nowell, &c.
Then to Bethlem town
We went two and two,
And in a sorry place
Heard the oxen low.
Nowell, &c.

Therein did we see
A sweet and goodly May,
And a fair old man;
Upon the straw she lay.
Nowell, &c.

And a little CHILD
On her arm had she;
'Wot ye who this is?'
Said the hinds to me.
Nowell, &c.

Ox and ass him know,
Kneeling on their knee:
Wondrous joy had I
This little BABE to see.
Nowell, &c.

This is CHRIST the Lord,
Masters, be ye glad!
Christmas is come in,
And no folk should be sad.
Nowell, &c.

THE ADORATION OF THE WISE MEN
CECIL FRANCES ALEXANDER

Saw you never in the twilight,
When the sun had left the skies,
Up in heaven the clear stars shining,
Through the gloom like silver eyes?
So of old the wise men watching,
Saw a little stranger star,
And they knew the King was given,
And they follow'd it from far.

Heard you never of the story,
How they cross'd the desert wild,
Journey'd on by plain and mountain,
Till they found the Holy Child?
How they open'd all their treasure,
Kneeling to that Infant King,
Gave the gold and fragrant incense,
Gave the myrrh in offering?

Know ye not that lowly Baby
Was the bright and morning star,
He who came to light the Gentiles,
And the darken'd isles afar?
And we too may seek his cradle,
There our heart's best treasures bring,
Love, and Faith, and true devotion,
For our Saviour, God, and King.

THE SHEPHERDS IN JUDEA
MARY AUSTIN

Oh, the Shepherds in Judea,
They are pacing to and fro,
For the air grows chill at twilight
And the weanling lambs are slow!

Leave, O lambs, the dripping sedges, quit the bramble and the
brier,
Leave the fields of barley stubble, for we light the watching fire;
Twinkling fires across the twilight, and a bitter watch to keep,
Lest the prowlers come a-thieving where the flocks unguarded
sleep.

Oh, the Shepherds in Judea,
They are singing soft and low—
Song the blessed angels taught them
All the centuries ago!

There was never roof to hide them, there were never walls to
bind;
Stark they lie beneath the star-beams, whom the blessed angels
find,
With the huddled flocks upstarting, wondering if they hear
aright,
While the Kings come riding, riding, solemn shadows in the
night.

Oh, the Shepherds in Judea,
They are thinking, as they go,
Of the light that broke their watching
On the hillside in the snow!—

Scattered snow along the hillside, white as springtime fleeces

are,
With the whiter wings above them and the glory-streaming
star—
Guiding-star across the housetops; never fear the Shepherds
felt
Till they found the Babe in manger where the kindly cattle knelt.

Oh, the Shepherds in Judea!—
Do you think the Shepherds know
How the whole round earth is brightened
In the ruddy Christmas glow?

How the sighs are lost in laughter, and the laughter brings the
tears,
As the thoughts of men go seeking back across the darkling
years
Till they find the wayside stable that the star-led Wise Men
found,
With the Shepherds, mute, adoring, and the glory shining
round!

CHRISTMAS CAROL
JAMES S. PARK

So crowded was the little town
On the first Christmas day,
Tired Mary Mother laid her down
To rest upon the hay.
(Ah, would my door might have been thrown
Wide open on her way!)

But when the Holy Babe was born
In the deep hush of night,
It seemed as if a Sabbath morn
Had come with sacred light.
Child Jesus made the place forlorn
With his own beauty bright.

The manger rough was all his rest;
The cattle, having fed,
Stood silent by, or closer pressed,
And gravely wonderèd.
(Ah, Lord, if only that my breast
Had cradled Thee instead!)

NEIGHBORS OF THE CHRIST NIGHT
NORA ARCHIBALD SMITH

Deep in the shelter of the cave,
The ass with drooping head
Stood weary in the shadow, where
His master's hand had led.
About the manger oxen lay,
Bending a wide-eyed gaze
Upon the little new-born Babe,
Half worship, half amaze.
High in the roof the doves were set,
And cooed there, soft and mild,
Yet not so sweet as, in the hay,
The Mother to her Child.
The gentle cows breathed fragrant breath
To keep Babe Jesus warm,
While loud and clear, o'er hill and dale,
The cocks crowed, "Christ is born!"
Out in the fields, beneath the stars,
The young lambs sleeping lay,
And dreamed that in the manger slept
Another white as they.

- - - - -

These were Thy neighbors, Christmas Child;
To Thee their love was given,
For in Thy baby face there shone
The wonder-light of Heaven.

41

CRADLE HYMN
ISAAC WATTS

Hush, my dear, lie still and slumber;
Holy angels guard thy bed;
Heavenly blessings without number
Gently falling on thy head.

Sleep, my babe, thy food and raiment,
House and home, thy friends provide;
All without thy care, or payment,
All thy wants are well supplied.

How much better thou'rt attended
Than the Son of God could be,
When from heaven He descended,
And became a child like thee!

Soft and easy is thy cradle;
Coarse and hard thy Saviour lay,
When His birthplace was a stable,
And His softest bed was hay.

See the kindly shepherds round him,
Telling wonders from the sky!
When they sought Him, there they found Him,
With his Virgin-Mother by.

See the lovely babe a-dressing;
Lovely infant, how He smiled!
When He wept, the mother's blessing
Soothed and hushed the holy child.

Lo, He slumbers in His manger,
Where the honest oxen fed;

—Peace, my darling! here's no danger!
Here's no ox a-near thy bed!

Mayst thou live to know and fear Him,
Trust and love Him all thy days;
Then go dwell forever near Him,
See His face, and sing His praise!

I could give thee thousand kisses,
Hoping what I most desire;
Not a mother's fondest wishes
Can to greater joys aspire.

AN ODE ON THE BIRTH OF OUR SAVIOUR
ROBERT HERRICK

In numbers, and but these few,
I sing thy birth, O Jesu!
Thou pretty baby, born here
With sup'rabundant scorn here;
Who for thy princely port here,
Hadst for thy place
Of birth, a base
Out-stable for thy court here.

Instead of neat enclosures
Of interwoven osiers,
Instead of fragrant posies
Of daffodils and roses,
Thy cradle, kingly stranger,
As gospel tells,
Was nothing else
But here a homely manger.

But we with silks, not crewels,
With sundry precious jewels,
And lily work will dress thee,
And, as we dispossess thee
Of clouts, we'll make a chamber,
Sweet babe, for thee
Of ivory,
And plaster'd round with amber.

CHRISTMAS SONG
EDMUND HAMILTON SEARS
Calm on the listening ear of night
Come heaven's melodious strains,
Where wild Judea stretches far

Her silver-mantled plains;
Celestial choirs from courts above
Shed sacred glories there;
And angels with their sparkling lyres
Make music on the air.

The answering hills of Palestine
Send back the glad reply,
And greet from all their holy heights
The day-spring from on high:
O'er the blue depths of Galilee
There comes a holier calm,
And Sharon waves, in solemn praise,
Her silent groves of palm.

"Glory to God!" The lofty strain
The realm of ether fills:
How sweeps the song of solemn joy
O'er Judah's sacred hills!
"Glory to God!" The sounding skies
Loud with their anthems ring;
"Peace on the earth; good-will to men,
From heaven's eternal King!"

Light on thy hills, Jerusalem!
The Saviour now is born:
More bright on Bethlehem's joyous plains
Breaks the first Christmas morn;
And brighter on Moriah's brow,
Crowned with her temple-spires,
Which first proclaim the new-born light,
Clothed with its Orient fires.

This day shall Christian lips be mute,
And Christian hearts be cold?
Oh, catch the anthem that from heaven

O'er Judah's mountains rolled!
When nightly burst from seraph-harps
The high and solemn lay,—
"Glory to God! on earth be peace;
Salvation comes to-day!"

A HYMN ON THE NATIVITY OF MY SAVIOUR
BEN JONSON

I sing the birth was born to-night
The author both of life and light;
The angels so did sound it.
And like the ravished shepherds said,
Who saw the light, and were afraid,
Yet searched, and true they found it.

The Son of God, th' eternal king,
That did us all salvation bring,
And freed the soul from danger;
He whom the whole world could not take,
The Word, which heaven and earth did make,
Was now laid in a manger.

The Father's wisdom willed it so,
The Son's obedience knew no No,
Both wills were in one stature;
And as that wisdom had decreed,
The Word was now made flesh indeed,
And took on him our nature.

What comfort by him do we win,
Who made himself the price of sin,
To make us heirs of glory!
To see this babe all innocence;
A martyr born in our defence:
Can man forget the story?

THE SHEPHERD'S SONG
EDMUND BOLTON

Sweet music, sweeter far
Than any song is sweet:
Sweet music, heavenly rare,
Mine ears, O peers, doth greet.
You gentle flocks, whose fleeces pearled with dew,
Resemble heaven, whom golden drops make bright,
Listen, O listen, now, O not to you
Our pipes make sport to shorten weary night:
But voices most divine
Make blissful harmony:
Voices that seem to shine,
For what else clears the sky?
Tunes can we hear, but not the singers see,
The tunes divine, and so the singers be.

Lo, how the firmament
Within an azure fold
The flock of stars hath pent,
That we might them behold,
Yet from their beams proceedeth not this light,
Nor can their crystals such reflection give.
What then doth make the element so bright?
The heavens are come down upon earth to live
But hearken to the song,
Glory to glory's King,
And peace all men among,
These quiristers do sing.
Angels they are, as also (shepherds) He
Whom in our fear we do admire to see.

Let not amazement blind
Your souls, said he, annoy:

To you and all mankind
My message bringeth joy.
For lo! the world's great Shepherd now is born,
A blessed Babe, an Infant full of power:
After long night uprisen is the morn,
Renowning Bethlem in the Saviour.
Sprung is the perfect day,
By prophets seen afar:
Sprung is the mirthful May,
Which winter cannot mar.
In David's city doth this Sun appear
Clouded in flesh, yet, shepherds, sit we here!

A CHRISTMAS CAROL
AUBREY DE VERE

They leave the land of gems and gold,
   The shining portals of the East;
For Him, the woman's Seed foretold,
   They leave the revel and the feast.

To earth their sceptres they have cast,
   And crowns by kings ancestral worn;
They track the lonely Syrian waste;
   They kneel before the Babe new born.

O happy eyes that saw Him first;
   O happy lips that kissed His feet:
Earth slakes at last her ancient thirst;
   With Eden's joy her pulses beat.

True kings are those who thus forsake
   Their kingdoms for the Eternal King;
   Serpent, her foot is on thy neck;
Herod, thou writhest, but canst not sting.
   He, He is King, and He alone
   Who lifts that infant hand to bless;
Who makes His mother's knee His throne,
   Yet rules the starry wilderness.

A CHRISTMAS HYMN
ANON

Written in the Chapel of the Manger, in the Convent Church of
Bethlehem, Palestine:
In the fields where, long ago,
Dropping tears, amid the leaves,
Ruth's young feet went to and fro,
Binding up the scattered sheaves,
In the field that heard the voice
Of Judea's shepherd King,
Still the gleaners may rejoice,
Still the reapers shout and sing.

For each mount and vale and plain
Felt the touch of holier feet.
Then the gleaners of the grain
Heard, in voices full and sweet,
"Peace on earth, good will to men,"
Ring from angel lips afar,
While, o'er every glade and glen,
Broke the light of Bethlehem's star.

Star of hope to souls in night,
Star of peace above our strife,
Guiding, where the gates of death
Ope to fields of endless life.
Wanderer from the nightly throng
Which the eastern heavens gem;
Guided, by an angel's song,
To the Babe of Bethlehem.

Not Judea's hills alone
Have earth's weary gleaners trod,
Not to heirs of David's throne

Is it given to "reign with God."
But where'er on His green earth
Heavenly faith and longing are,
Heavenly hope and life have birth,
'Neath the smile of Bethlehem's star.

In each lowly heart or home,
By each love-watched cradle-bed,
Where we rest, or where we roam,
Still its changeless light is shed.
In its beams each quickened heart,
Howe'er saddened or denied,
Keeps one little place apart
For the Hebrew mother's Child.

And that inner temple fair
May be holier ground than this,
Hallowed by the pilgrim's prayer,
Warmed by many a pilgrim's kiss.
In its shadow still and dim,
Where our holiest longings are,
Rings forever Bethlehem's hymn,
Shines forever Bethlehem's star.

CHRISTMAS DAY
CHARLES WESLEY
Hark! the herald angels sing
Glory to the new-born King!
Peace on earth and mercy mild,
God and sinners reconciled.

Joyful all ye nations rise,
Join the triumph of the skies,
With the angelic host proclaim
Christ is born in Bethlehem!

Hail the heaven-born Prince of Peace!
Hail the Sun of Righteousness!
Light and life to all he brings,
Risen with healing in his wings.

Mild, he lays his glory by;
Born, that man no more may die,
Born to raise the sons of earth,
Born to give them second birth.

CHRISTMAS
ANON

Once in Royal David's city
Stood a lowly cattle shed,
Where a mother laid her baby
In a manger for His bed.
Mary was that mother mild,
Jesus Christ that little child.

He came down to earth from Heaven,
Who is God and Lord of all.
And his shelter was a stable,
And his cradle was a stall.
With the poor and mean and lowly,
Lived on earth our Saviour Holy.

And our eyes at last shall see Him
Through His own redeeming love,
For that child so dear and gentle
Is our Lord in Heaven above;
And He leads His children on
To the place where He is gone.

Not in that poor, lowly stable,
With the oxen standing by,
We shall see Him; but in Heaven,
Set at God's right hand on high,
When, like stars, His children crowned
All in white, shall wait around.

CHRISTMAS
NAHUM TATE

While shepherds watch'd their flocks by night,
All seated on the ground,
The angel of the Lord came down,
And glory shone around.

"Fear not," said he (for mighty dread
Had seized their troubled mind);
"Glad tidings of great joy I bring
To you and all mankind.

"To you, in David's town, this day
Is born of David's line
The Saviour who is Christ the Lord;
And this shall be the sign:

"The heavenly Babe you there shall find
To human view display'd,
All meanly wrapt in swathing bands,
And in a manger laid."

Thus spake the Seraph; and forthwith
Appear'd a shining throng
Of angels, praising God, and thus
Address'd their joyful song:

"All glory be to God on high,
And to the earth be peace;
Good-will henceforth from heaven to men
Begin, and never cease!"

"WHILE SHEPHERDS WATCHED THEIR FLOCKS BY NIGHT"
MARGARET DELAND

Like small curled feathers, white and soft,
The little clouds went by,
Across the moon, and past the stars,
And down the western sky:
In upland pastures, where the grass
With frosted dew was white,
Like snowy clouds the young sheep lay,
That first, best Christmas night.

The shepherds slept; and, glimmering faint,
With twist of thin, blue smoke,
Only their fire's crackling flames
The tender silence broke—
Save when a young lamb raised his head,
Or, when the night wind blew,
A nesting bird would softly stir,
Where dusky olives grew—

With finger on her solemn lip,
Night hushed the shadowy earth,
And only stars and angels saw
The little Saviour's birth;
Then came such flash of silver light
Across the bending skies,
The wondering shepherds woke, and hid
Their frightened, dazzled eyes!

And all their gentle sleepy flock
Looked up, then slept again,
Nor knew the light that dimmed the stars
Brought endless Peace to men—
Nor even heard the gracious words

That down the ages ring—
The Christ is born! the Lord has come,
Good-will on earth to bring!

Then o'er the moonlit, misty fields,
Dumb with the world's great joy,
The shepherds sought the white-walled town,
Where lay the baby boy—
And oh, the gladness of the world,
The glory of the skies,
Because the longed-for Christ looked up
In Mary's happy eyes!

COLONIAL CHRISTMASES
ALICE MORSE EARLE

[From "Customs and Fashions in Old New England."]
The first century of colonial life saw few set times and days for pleasure. The holy days of the English Church were as a stench to the Puritan nostrils, and their public celebration was at once rigidly forbidden by the laws of New England. New holidays were not quickly evolved, and the sober gatherings for matters of Church and State for a time took their place. The hatred of "wanton Bacchanallian Christmasses" spent throughout England, as Cotton said, in "revelling, dicing, carding, masking, mumming, consumed in compotations, in interludes, in excess of wine, in mad mirth," was the natural reaction of intelligent and thoughtful minds against the excesses of a festival which had ceased to be a Christian holiday, but was dominated by a lord of misrule who did not hesitate to invade the churches in time of service, in his noisy revels and sports. English Churchmen long ago revolted also against such Christmas observance.

Of the first Pilgrim Christmas we know but little, save that it was spent, as was many a later one, in work....

By 1659 the Puritans had grown to hate Christmas more and more; it was, to use Shakespeare's words, "the bug that feared them all." The very name smacked to them of incense, stole, and monkish jargon; any person who observed it as a holiday by forbearing of labor, feasting, or any other way was to pay five shillings fine, so desirous were they to "beate down every sprout of Episcopacie." Judge Sewall watched jealously the feeling of the people with regard to Christmas, and noted with pleasure on each succeeding year the continuance of common traffic throughout the day. Such entries as this show his attitude: "Dec. 25, 1685. Carts come to town and shops open as usual. Some somehow observe the day, but are vexed I believe that the Body of people profane it, and blessed be God no authority yet to compel them to keep it." When the Church of England established Christmas services in Boston a few years later, we find the Judge waging hopeless war against Governor Belcher over it, and hear him praising his son for not going with other boy friends to hear the novel and attractive services. He says: "I dehort mine from Christmas keeping and charge them to forbear."

Christmas could not be regarded till this century as a New England holiday, though in certain localities, such as old Narragansett—an opulent community which was settled by Episcopalians—two weeks of Christmas visiting and feasting were entered into with zest by both planters and slaves for many years previous to the revolution.

THE ANGELS
WILLIAM DRUMMOND

Run, shepherds, run where Bethlehem blest appears.
We bring the best of news; be not dismayed:
A Saviour there is born more old than years,
Amidst heaven's rolling height this earth who stayed.

In a poor cottage inned, a virgin maid,
A weakling did him bear, who all upbears;
There is he poorly swaddled, in manger laid,
To whom too narrow swaddlings are our spheres:
Run, shepherds, run, and solemnize his birth.

This is that night—no, day, grown great with bliss,
In which the power of Satan broken is:
In heaven be glory, peace unto the earth!
Thus singing, through the air the angels swarm,
And cope of stars re-echoèd the same.

Or say, if this new Birth of ours
Sleeps, laid within some ark of flowers,
Spangled with dew-light; thou canst clear
All doubts, and manifest the where.

Declare to us, bright star, if we shall seek
Him in the morning's blushing cheek,
Or search the beds of spices through,
To find him out?

Star.—No, this ye need not do;
But only come and see Him rest,
A princely babe, in's mother's breast.

HYMN FOR CHRISTMAS

FELICIA HEMANS

Oh! lovely voices of the sky
Which hymned the Saviour's birth,
Are ye not singing still on high,
Ye that sang, "Peace on earth"?
To us yet speak the strains
Wherewith, in time gone by,
Ye blessed the Syrian swains,
Oh! voices of the sky!

Oh! clear and shining light, whose beams
That hour Heaven's glory shed,
Around the palms, and o'er the streams,
And on the shepherd's head.
Be near, through life and death,
As in that holiest night
Of hope, and joy, and faith—
Oh! clear and shining light!

NEW PRINCE, NEW POMP
ROBERT SOUTHWELL

Behold a simple, tender Babe,
In freezing winter night,
In homely manger trembling lies;
Alas! a piteous sight.

The inns are full; no man will yield
This little Pilgrim bed;
But forced he is with silly beasts
In crib to shroud his head.

Despise him not for lying there;
First what he is inquire:
An Orient pearl is often found
In depth of dirty mire.

Weigh not his crib, his wooden dish,
Nor beasts that by him feed;
Weigh not his mother's poor attire,
Nor Joseph's simple weed.

This stable is a Prince's court,
The crib his chair of state;
The beasts are parcel of his pomp,
The wooden dish his plate.

The persons in that poor attire
His royal liveries wear;
The Prince himself is come from heaven:
This pomp is praisèd there.

With joy approach, O Christian wight!
Do homage to thy King;

And highly praise this humble pomp,
Which he from heaven doth bring.

THE THREE KINGS
HENRY WADSWORTH LONGFELLOW

Three Kings came riding from far away,
Melchior and Gaspar and Baltasar;
Three Wise Men out of the East were they,
And they traveled by night and they slept by day,
For their guide was a beautiful, wonderful star.

The star was so beautiful, large and clear,
That all the other stars of the sky
Became a white mist in the atmosphere;
And by this they knew that the coming was near
Of the Prince foretold in the prophecy.

Three caskets they bore on their saddle-bows,
Three caskets of gold with golden keys;
Their robes were of crimson silk, with rows
Of bells and pomegranates and furbelows,
Their turbans like blossoming almond-trees.

And so the Three Kings rode into the West,
Through the dusk of night over hill and dell,
And sometimes they nodded with beard on breast,
And sometimes talked, as they paused to rest,
With the people they met at some wayside well.

"Of the child that is born," said Baltasar,
"Good people, I pray you, tell us the news;
For we in the East have seen his star,
And have ridden fast, and have ridden far,
To find and worship the King of the Jews."

And the people answered, "You ask in vain;
We know of no king but Herod the Great!"

They thought the Wise Men were men insane,
As they spurred their horses across the plain
Like riders in haste who cannot wait.

And when they came to Jerusalem,
Herod the Great, who had heard this thing,
Sent for the Wise Men and questioned them;
And said, "Go down unto Bethlehem,
And bring me tidings of this new king."

So they rode away, and the star stood still,
The only one in the gray of morn;
Yes, it stopped, it stood still of its own free will,
Right over Bethlehem on the hill,
The city of David where Christ was born.

And the Three Kings rode through the gate and the guard,
Through the silent street, till their horses turned
And neighed as they entered the great inn-yard;
But the windows were closed, and the doors were barred,
And only a light in the stable burned.

And cradled there in the scented hay,
In the air made sweet by the breath of kine,
The little child in the manger lay,
The Child that would be King one day
Of a kingdom not human, but divine.

His mother, Mary of Nazareth,
Sat watching beside his place of rest,
Watching the even flow of his breath,
For the joy of life and the terror of death
Were mingled together in her breast.

They laid their offerings at his feet:
The gold was their tribute to a King;

The frankincense, with its odor sweet,
Was for the Priest, the Paraclete;
The myrrh for the body's burying.

And the mother wondered and bowed her head,
And sat as still as a statue of stone;
Her heart was troubled yet comforted,
Remembering what the angel had said
Of an endless reign and of David's throne.

Then the Kings rode out of the city gate,
With a clatter of hoofs in proud array;
But they went not back to Herod the Great,
For they knew his malice and feared his hate,
And returned to their homes by another way.

HYMN ON THE NATIVITY
JOHN MILTON

It was the winter wild,
While the heaven-born child
All meanly wrapt in the rude manger lies;
Nature, in awe of him,
Had doffed her gaudy trim,
With her great Master so to sympathize:
It was no season then for her
To wanton with the sun, her lusty paramour.

Only with speeches fair
She wooes the gentle air,
To hide her guilty front with innocent snow;
And on her naked shame,
Pollute with sinful blame,
The saintly veil of maiden-white to throw;
Confounded, that her Maker's eyes
Should look so near upon her foul deformities.

But he, her fears to cease,
Sent down the meek-eyed Peace:
She, crowned with olive green, came softly sliding
Down through the turning sphere,
His ready harbinger,
With turtle wing the amorous clouds dividing;
And, waving wide her myrtle wand,
She strikes a universal peace through sea and land.

No war or battle's sound
Was heard the world around:
The idle spear and shield were high uphung;
The hookèd chariot stood
Unstained with hostile blood;

The trumpet spake not to the armèd throng;
And kings sat still with awful eye,
As if they surely knew their sovereign lord was by.

But peaceful was the night,
Wherein the Prince of Light
His reign of peace upon the earth began:
The winds, with wonder whist,
Smoothly the waters kissed,
Whispering new joys to the mild ocean,
Who now hath quite forgot to rave,
While birds of calm sit brooding on the charmèd wave.

The stars, with deep amaze,
Stand fixed in steadfast gaze,
Bending one way their precious influence;
And will not take their flight,
For all the morning light,
Or Lucifer had often warned them thence:
But in their glimmering orbs did glow,
Until their Lord himself bespake, and bid them go.

And, though the shady gloom
Had given day her room,
The sun himself withheld his wonted speed,
And hid his head for shame.
As his inferior flame
The new-enlightened world no more should need;
He saw a greater sun appear
Than his bright throne, or burning axletree, could bear.

The shepherds on the lawn,
Or ere the point of dawn,
Sat simply chatting in a rustic row;
Full little thought they then
That the mighty Pan

Was kindly come to live with them below;
Perhaps their loves, or else their sheep,
Was all that did their silly thoughts so busy keep.

When such music sweet
Their hearts and ears did greet,
As never was by mortal fingers strook,
Divinely warbled voice
Answering the stringèd noise,
As all their souls in blissful rapture took:
The air, such pleasure loath to lose,
With thousand echoes still prolongs each heavenly close.

Nature, that heard such sound,
Beneath the hollow round
Of Cynthia's seat, the airy region thrilling,
Now was almost won,
To think her part was done,
And that her reign had here its last fulfilling;
She knew such harmony alone
Could hold all heaven and earth in happier union.

At last surrounds their sight
A globe of circular light,
That with long beams the shame-faced night arrayed;
The helmèd cherubim,
And sworded seraphim,
Are seen in glittering ranks with wings displayed,
Harping in loud and solemn quire,
With unexpressive notes, to Heaven's new-born heir.

Such music as 'tis said
Before was never made,
But when of old the sons of morning sung,
While the Creator great
His constellations set,

And the well-balanced world on hinges hung,
And cast the dark foundations deep,
And bid the weltering waves their oozy channel keep.

Ring out, ye crystal spheres,
Once bless our human ears,
If ye have power to touch our senses so;
And let your silver chime
Move in melodious time;
And let the bass of Heaven's deep organ blow;
And, with your ninefold harmony,
Make up full concert to the angelic symphony.

For, if such holy song
Enwrap our fancy long,
Time will run back, and fetch the age of gold;
And speckled Vanity
Will sicken soon and die,
And leprous Sin will melt from earthly mould;
And Hell itself will pass away,
And leave her dolorous mansions to the peering day.

Yea, Truth and Justice then
Will down return to men,
Orbed in a rainbow; and, like glories wearing,
Mercy will sit between,
Throned in celestial sheen,
With radiant feet the tissued clouds down steering;
And Heaven, as at some festival,
Will open wide the gates of her high palace hall.

But wisest Fate says no,
This must not yet be so;
The babe yet lies in smiling infancy,
That on the bitter cross
Must redeem our loss,

So both himself and us to glorify:
Yet first, to those chained in sleep,
The wakeful trump of doom must thunder through the deep,

With such a horrid clang
As on Mount Sinai rang,
While the red fire and smouldering clouds outbrake;
The aged earth aghast,
With terror of that blast,
Shall from the surface to the centre shake;
When, at the world's last session,
The dreadful Judge in middle air shall spread his throne.

And then at last our bliss,
Full and perfect is,
But now begins; for, from this happy day,
The old dragon, underground,
In straiter limits bound,
Not half so far casts his usurpèd sway;
And, wroth to see his kingdom fail,
Swinges the scaly horror of his folded tail.

The oracles are dumb;
No voice or hideous hum
Runs through the archèd roof in words deceiving.
Apollo from his shrine
Can no more divine,
With hollow shriek the steep of Delphos leaving.
No nightly trance, or breathèd spell,
Inspires the pale-eyed priest from the prophetic cell.

The lonely mountains o'er,
And the resounding shore,
A voice of weeping heard and loud lament;
From haunted spring and dale,
Edged with poplar pale,

71

The parting Genius is with sighing sent;
With flower-inwoven tresses torn,
The nymphs in twilight shade of tangled thickets mourn.

In consecrated earth,
And on the holy hearth,
The Lars and Lemures mourn with midnight plaint.
In urns and altars round,
A drear and dying sound
Affrights the Flamens at their service quaint;
And the chill marble seems to sweat,
While each peculiar power foregoes his wonted seat.

Peor and Baälim
Forsake their temples dim
With that twice-battered God of Palestine;
And moonèd Ashtaroth
Heaven's queen and mother both,
Now sits not girt with tapers' holy shine;
The Libyac Hammon shrinks his horn;
In vain the Tyrian maids their wounded Thammuz mourn.

And sullen Moloch, fled,
Hath left in shadows dread
His burning idol all of blackest hue:
In vain with cymbals' ring
They call the grisly king,
In dismal dance about the furnace blue:
The brutish gods of Nile as fast,
Isis, and Orus, and the dog Anubis, haste.

Nor is Osiris seen
In Memphian grove or green,
Trampling the unshowered grass with lowings loud;
Nor can he be at rest
Within his sacred chest,

Naught but profoundest hell can be his shroud;
In vain with timbrelled anthems dark
The sable-stolèd sorcerers bear his worshipped ark.

He feels from Judah's land
The dreaded infant's hand,
The rays of Bethlehem blind his dusky eyne;
Nor all the gods beside
Longer dare abide,
Not Typhon huge ending in snaky twine;
Our babe, to show his Godhead true,
Can in his swaddling bands control the damnèd crew.

So, when the sun in bed,
Curtained with cloudy red,
Pillows his chin upon an orient wave,
The flocking shadows pale
Troop to the infernal jail,
Each fettered ghost slips to his several grave;
And the yellow-skirted fays
Fly after the night-steeds, leaving their moon-loved maze.

But see, the Virgin blest
Hath laid her babe to rest;
Time is our tedious song should here have ending:
Heaven's youngest-teèmed star
Hath fixed her polished car,
Her sleeping Lord with handmaid lamp attending;
And all about the courtly stable
Bright-harnessed angels sit in order serviceable.

II
CELEBRATION
CHRISTMAS EVE AT MR. WARDLE'S
From "Pickwick Papers"
CHARLES DICKENS

From the center of the ceiling of this kitchen, old Wardle had just suspended with his own hands a huge branch of mistletoe, and this same branch of mistletoe instantaneously gave rise to a scene of general and most delightful struggling and confusion; in the midst of which Mr. Pickwick with a gallantry which would have done honour to a descendant of Lady Trollimglower herself, took the old lady by the hand, led her beneath the mystic branch, and saluted her in all courtesy and decorum. The old lady submitted to this piece of practical politeness with all the dignity which befitted so important and serious a solemnity, but the younger ladies not being so thoroughly imbued with a superstitious veneration of the custom, or imagining that the value of a salute is very much enhanced if it cost a little trouble to obtain it, screamed and struggled, and ran into corners, and threatened and remonstrated, and did everything but leave the room, until some of the less adventurous gentlemen were on the point of desisting, when they all at once found it useless to resist any longer, and submitted to be kissed with a good grace. Mr. Winkle kissed the young lady with the black eyes, and Mr. Snodgrass kissed Emily; and Mr. Weller, not being particular about the form of being under the mistletoe, kissed Emma and the other female servants, just as he caught them. As to the poor relations, they kissed everybody, not even excepting the plainer portion of the young-lady visitors, who, in their excessive confusion, ran right under the mistletoe, directly it was hung up, without knowing it! Wardle stood with his back to the fire, surveying the whole scene, with the utmost satisfaction; and the fat boy took the opportunity of appropriating to his own use, and summarily devouring, a particularly fine mince-pie, that had been carefully put by for somebody else.

Now the screaming had subsided, and faces were in a glow and curls in a tangle, and Mr. Pickwick, after kissing the old lady as before mentioned, was standing under the mistletoe, looking with a very pleased countenance on all that was passing around him, when the young lady with the black eyes, after a little whispering with the other young ladies, made a sudden dart forward, and, putting her arm around Mr. Pickwick's neck, saluted him affectionately on the left cheek; and before Mr. Pickwick distinctly knew what was the matter, he was surrounded by the whole body, and kissed by every one of them.

It was a pleasant thing to see Mr. Pickwick in the centre of the group, now pulled this way, and then that, and first kissed on the chin and then on the nose, and then on the spectacles, and to hear the peals of laughter which were raised on every side; but it was a still more pleasant thing to see Mr. Pickwick, blinded shortly afterwards with a silk-handkerchief, falling up against the wall, and scrambling into corners, and going through all the mysteries of blind-man's buff, with the utmost relish of the game, until at last he caught one of the poor relations; and then had to evade the blind-man himself, which he did with a nimbleness and agility that elicited the admiration and applause of all beholders. The poor relations caught just the people whom they thought would like it; and when the game flagged, got caught themselves. When they were all tired of blind-man's buff, there was a great game at snapdragon, and when fingers enough were burned with that, and all the raisons gone, they sat down by the huge fire of blazing logs to a substantial supper, and a mighty bowl of wassail, something smaller than an ordinary washhouse copper, in which the hot apples were hissing and bubbling with a rich look, and a jolly sound, that were perfectly irresistible.

"This," said Mr. Pickwick, looking round him, "this is, indeed, comfort."

75

"Our invariable custom," replied Mr. Wardle. "Everybody sits down with us on Christmas eve, as you see them now—servants and all; and here we wait till the clock strikes twelve, to usher Christmas in, and wile away the time with forfeits and old stories. Trundle, my boy, rake up the fire."

Up flew the bright sparks in myriads as the logs were stirred, and the deep red blaze sent forth a rich glow, that penetrated into the furthest corner of the room, and cast its cheerful tint on every face.

"Come," said Wardle, "a song—a Christmas song. I'll give you one, in default of a better."

"Bravo," said Mr. Pickwick.

"Fill up," cried Wardle. "It will be two hours good, before you see the bottom of the bowl through the deep rich colour of the wassail; fill up all round, and now for the song."

Thus saying, the merry old gentleman, in a good, round, sturdy voice, commenced without more ado—

A CHRISTMAS CAROL

I care not for Spring; on his fickle wing
Let the blossoms and buds be borne:
He woos them amain with his treacherous rain,
And he scatters them ere the morn.
An inconstant elf, he knows not himself,
Or his own changing mind an hour,
He'll smile in your face, and, with wry grimace,
He'll wither your youngest flower.

Let the summer sun to his bright home run,
He shall never be sought by me;
When he's dimmed by a cloud I can laugh aloud,
And care not how sulky he be;
For his darling child is the madness wild
That sports in fierce fever's train;
And when love is too strong, it don't last long,
As many have found to their pain.

A mild harvest night, by the tranquil light
Of the modest and gentle moon,
Has a far sweeter sheen for me, I ween,
Than the broad and unblushing noon,
But every leaf awakens my grief,
As it lieth beneath the tree;
So let Autumn air be never so fair,
It by no means agrees with me.

But my song I troll out, for Christmas stout,
The hearty, the true, and the bold;
A bumper I drain, and with might and main
Give three cheers for this Christmas old.
We'll usher him in with a merry din
That shall gladden his joyous heart,
And we'll keep him up while there's bite or sup,

And in fellowship good, we'll part.

In his fine honest pride, he scorns to hide
One jot of his hard-weather scars;
They're no disgrace, for there's much the same trace
On the cheeks of our bravest tars.
Then again I sing 'till the roof doth ring,
And it echoes from wall to wall—
To the stout old wight, fair welcome to-night,
As the King of the Seasons all!

A VISIT FROM ST. NICHOLAS
CLEMENT C. MOORE

'Twas the night before Christmas, when all through the house
Not a creature was stirring, not even a mouse;
The stockings were hung by the chimney with care,
In hopes that St. Nicholas soon would be there;
The children were nestled all snug in their beds,
While visions of sugar-plums danced through their heads;
And mamma in her kerchief, and I in my cap,
Had just settled our brains for a long winter's nap,—
When out on the lawn there arose such a clatter,
I sprang from my bed to see what was the matter.
Away to the window I flew like a flash,
Tore open the shutters and threw up the sash.
The moon, on the breast of the new-fallen snow,
Gave a lustre of midday to objects below;
When what to my wondering eyes should appear,
But a miniature sleigh and eight tiny reindeer,
With a little old driver, so lively and quick
I knew in a moment it must be St. Nick.
More rapid than eagles his coursers they came,
And he whistled and shouted and called them by name:
"Now, Dasher! now, Dancer! now, Prancer and Vixen!
On, Comet! on, Cupid! on, Donder and Blitzen!
To the top of the porch, to the top of the wall!
Now, dash away, dash away, dash away all!"
As dry leaves that before the wild hurricane fly,
When they meet with an obstacle, mount to the sky,
So, up to the house-top the coursers they flew,
With a sleigh full of toys,—and St. Nicholas too.
And then in a twinkling I heard on the roof
The prancing and pawing of each little hoof,
As I drew in my head and was turning around,
Down the chimney St. Nicholas came with a bound.
He was dressed all in fur from his head to his foot,

And his clothes were all tarnished with ashes and soot;
A bundle of toys he had flung on his back,
And he looked like a pedler just opening his pack.
His eyes how they twinkled! his dimples how merry!
His cheeks were like roses, his nose like a cherry;
His droll little mouth was drawn up like a bow,
And the beard on his chin was as white as the snow.
The stump of a pipe he held tight in his teeth,
And the smoke it encircled his head like a wreath.
He had a broad face, and a little round belly
That shook, when he laughed, like a bowl full of jelly.
He was chubby and plump,—a right jolly old elf—
And I laughed when I saw him, in spite of myself.
A wink of his eye and a twist of his head
Soon gave me to know I had nothing to dread.
He spoke not a word, but went straight to his work,
And filled all the stockings; then turned with a jerk,
And laying his finger aside of his nose,
And giving a nod, up the chimney he rose.
He sprang to his sleigh, to his team gave a whistle,
And away they all flew like the down of a thistle;
But I heard him exclaim, ere he drove out of sight:
"Happy Christmas to all, and to all a good-night!"

A CHRISTMAS PIECE

Of garnered rhyme, from hidden stores of olden time that since the language did begin, have welcomed merry Christmas in, and made the winter nights so long, fleet by on wings of wine and song; for when the snow is on the roof, the house within is sorrow proof, if yule log blazes on the hearth, and cups and hearts o'er-brim with mirth. Then bring the wassail to the board, with nuts and fruit—the winter's hoard; and bid the children take off shoe, to hang their stockings by the flue; and let the clear and frosty sky, set out its brightest jewelry, to show old Santa Claus the road, so he may ease his gimcrack load. And with the coming of these times, we'll add some old and lusty rhymes, that suit the festive season well, and sound as sweet as Christmas bell.

Now just bethink of castle gate, where humble midnight mummers wait, to try if voices, one and all, can rouse the tipsy seneschal, to give them bread and beer and brawn, for tidings of the Christmas morn; or bid each yelper clear his throat, with water of the castle moat, for thus they used, by snow and torch, to rear their voices at the porch:

Fred S. Cozzens

WASSAILER'S SONG
ROBERT SOUTHWELL

Wassail! wassail! all over the town,
Our toast it is white, and our ale it is brown;
Our bowl is made of a maplin tree;
We be good fellows all;—I drink to thee.

Here's to our horse, and to his right ear,
God send master a happy new year;
A happy new year as e'er he did see,—
With my wassailing bowl I drink to thee.

Here's to our mare, and to her right eye,
God send our mistress a good Christmas pie;
A good Christmas pie as e'er I did see,—
With my wassailing bowl I drink to thee.

Here's to our cow, and to her long tail,
God send our measter us never may fail
Of a cup of good beer: I pray you draw near,
And our jolly wassail it's then you shall hear.

Be here any maids? I suppose here be some;
Sure they will not let young men stand on the cold stone!
Sing hey O, maids! come trole back the pin,
And the fairest maid in the house let us all in.

Come, butler, come, bring us a bowl of the best;
I hope your soul in heaven will rest;
But if you do bring us a bowl of the small,
Then down fall butler, and bowl and all.

- - - - -

And here's a Christmas carol meant for children, and most
excellent, and though the monk that wrote it was hung, yet still
his verses may be sung.

A CAROL

As I in a hoarie winter's night
Stood shivering in the snow,
Surpriz'd I was with sudden heat,
Which made my heart to glow;
And lifting up a fearefull eye
To view what fire was neere,
A prettie babe, all burning bright,
Did in the aire appeare;
Who, scorchèd with excessive heat,
Such flouds of teares did shed,
As though his flouds should quench his flames,
Which with his teares were bred:

Alas! (quoth he) but newly borne,
In fierie heats I frie,
Yet none approach to warm their hearts,
Or feele my fire, but I;
My faultless brest the furnace is,
The fuell, wounding thornes:
Love is the fire, and sighs the smoke,
The ashes, shames and scornes;
The fuell justice layeth on,
And mercy blows the coales,
The metalls in this furnace wrought,
Are Men's defiled soules:
For which, as now on fire I am,
To work them to their good,
So will I melt into a bath,
To wash them in my blood.
With this he vanisht out of sight,
And swiftly shrunke away,
And straight I called unto minde
That it was Christmasse Day.

CHRISTMAS EVE
HAMILTON WRIGHT MABIE
[From "My Study Fire."]

The world has been full of mysteries to-day; everybody has gone about weighted with secrets. The children's faces have fairly shone with expectancy, and I enter easily into the universal dream which at this moment holds all the children of Christendom under its spell. Was there ever a wider or more loving conspiracy than that which keeps the venerable figure of Santa Claus from slipping away, with all the other oldtime myths, into the forsaken wonderland of the past? Of all the personages whose marvelous doings once filled the minds of men, he alone survives. He has outlived all the great gods, and all the impressive and poetic conceptions which once flitted between heaven and earth; these have gone, but Santa Claus remains by virtue of a common understanding that childhood shall not be despoiled of one of its most cherished beliefs, either by the mythologist, with his sun myth theory, or the scientist, with his heartless diatribe against superstition. There is a good deal more to be said on this subject, if this were the place to say it; even superstition has its uses, and sometimes, its sound heart of truth. He who does not see in the legend of Santa Claus a beautiful faith on one side, and the naive embodiment of a divine fact on the other, is not fit to have a place at the Christmas board. For him there should be neither carol, nor holly, nor mistletoe; they only shall keep the feast to whom all these things are but the outward and visible signs of an inward and spiritual grace.

Rosalind and myself are thoroughly orthodox when it comes to the keeping of holidays; here at least the ways of our fathers are our ways also. Orthodoxy generally consists in retaining and emphasizing the disagreeable ways of the fathers, and as we are both inclined to heterodoxy on these points, we make the more

84

prominent our observance of the best of the old-time habits. I might preach a pleasant little sermon just here, taking as my text the "survival of the fittest," and illustrating the truth from our own domestic ritual; but the season preaches its own sermon, and I should only follow the example of some ministers and get between the text and my congregation if I made the attempt. For weeks we have all been looking forward to this eventful evening, and the still more eventful morrow. There have been hurried and whispered conferences hastily suspended at the sound of a familiar step on the stair; packages of every imaginable size and shape have been surreptitiously introduced into the house, and have immediately disappeared in all manner of out-of-the-way places; and for several weeks past one room has been constantly under lock and key, visited only when certain sharp-sighted eyes were occupied in other directions. Through all this scene of mystery Rosalind has moved sedately and with sealed lips, the common confidant of all the conspirators, and herself the greatest conspirator of all. Blessed is the season which engages the whole world in a conspiracy of love!

After dinner, eaten, let it be confessed, with more haste and less accompaniment of talk than usual, the parlor doors were opened, and there stood the Christmas tree in a glow of light, its wonderful branches laden with all manner of strange fruits not to be found in the botanies. The wild shouts, the merry laughter, the cries of delight as one coveted fruit after another dropped into long-expectant arms still linger in my ears now that the little tapers are burnt out, the boughs left bare, and the actors in the perennial drama are fast asleep, with new and strange bedfellows selected from the spoils of the night. Cradled between a delightful memory and a blissful anticipation, who does not envy them?

After this charming prelude is over, Rosalind comes into the study, and studies for the fortieth time the effect of the new design of decoration which she had this year worked out, and which gives these rather somber rows of books a homelike and festive aspect. It pleases me to note the spray of holly that obscures the title of Bacon's solemn and weighty "Essays," and I get half a page of suggestions for my notebook from the fact that a sprig of mistletoe has fallen on old Burton's "Anatomy of Melancholy." Rosalind has reason to be satisfied, and if I read her face aright she has succeeded even in her own eyes in bringing Christmas, with its fragrant memories and its heavenly visions, into the study. I cannot help thinking, as I watch her piling up the fire for a blaze of unusual splendor, that if more studies had their Rosalinds to bring in the genial currents of life there would be more cheer and hope and large-hearted wisdom in the books which the world is reading to-day.

When the fire has reached a degree of intensity and magnitude which Rosalind thinks adequate to the occasion, I take down a well-worn volume which opens of itself at a well-worn page. It is a book which I have read and re-read many times, and always with a kindling sympathy and affection for the man who wrote it; in whatever mood I take it up there is something in it which touches me with a sense of kinship. It is not a great book, but it is a book of the heart, and books of the heart have passed beyond the outer court of criticism before we bestow upon them that phrase of supreme regard. There are other books of the heart around me, but on Christmas Eve it is Alexander Smith's "Dreamthorp" which always seems to lie at my hand, and when I take it up the well-worn volume falls open at the essay on "Christmas." It is a good many years since Rosalind and I began to read together on Christmas Eve this beautiful meditation on the season, and now it has gathered about itself such a host of memories that it has become part of our common past. It is, indeed, a veritable palimpsest, overlaid with tender and gracious recollections out of which the original thought gains a new and subtle sweetness. As I read it aloud I know that she sees once more the familiar landscape about Dreamthorp, with the low, dark hill in the background, and over it "the tender radiance that precedes the moon"; the village windows are all lighted, and the "whole place shines like a

86

congregation of glowworms." There are the skaters still "leaning against the frosty wind"; there is the "gray church tower amid the leafless elms," around which the echoes of the morning peal of Christmas bells still hover; the village folk have gathered, "in their best dresses and their best faces"; the beautiful service of the church has been read and answered with heartfelt responses, the familiar story has been told again simply and urgently, with applications for every thankful soul, and then the congregation has gone to its homes and its festivities.

All these things, I am sure, lie within Rosalind's vision, although she seems to see nothing but the ruddy blaze of the fire; all these things I see, as I have seen them these many Christmas Eves agone; but with this familiar landscape there are mingled all the sweet and sorrowful memories of our common life, recalled at this hour that the light of the highest truth may interpret them anew in the divine language of hope. I read on until I come to the quotation from the "Hymn to the Nativity," and then I close the book, and take up a copy of Milton close at hand. We have had our commemoration service of love, and now there comes into our thought, with the organ roll of this sublime hymn, the universal truth which lies at the heart of the season. I am hardly conscious that it is my voice which makes these words audible: I am conscious only of this mighty-voiced anthem, fit for the choral song of the morning stars:

"Ring out, ye crystal spheres,
And bless our human ears,
If ye have power to touch our senses so;
And let your silver chime
Move in melodious time;
And let the bass of heaven's deep organ blow;
And, with your ninefold harmony,
Make up full concert to the angelic symphony.

"For, if such holy song
Enwrap our fancy long,
Time will run back and fetch the age of gold;

87

And speckled vanity
Will sicken soon and die,
And leprous sin will melt from earthly mold;
And hell itself will pass away,
And leave her dolorous mansions to the peering day.

- - - - -

"The oracles are dumb,
No voice or hideous hum
Runs through the archéd roof in words deceiving;
Apollo from his shrine
Can no more divine
With hollow shriek the steep of Delphos leaving,
No nightly trance or breathed spell
Inspires the pale-eyed priest from the prophetic cell.

"The lonely mountains o'er,
And the resounding shore,
A voice of weeping heard and loud lament;
From haunted spring, and dale
Edgéd with poplars pale,
The parting genius is with sighing sent;
With flower-enwoven tresses torn,
The nymphs in twilight shades of tangled thickets mourn."

- - - - -

Like a psalm the great Hymn fills the air, and like a psalm it
remains in the memory. The fire has burned low, and a soft and
solemn light fills the room. Neither of us speaks while the clock
strikes twelve. I look out of the window. The heavens are ablaze
with light, and somewhere amid those circling constellations I
know that a new star has found its place, and is shining with
such a ray as never before fell from heaven to earth.

CHRISTMAS IN THE OLDEN TIME
WALTER SCOTT

On Christmas-eve the bells were rung;
The damsel donned her kirtle sheen;
The hall was dressed with holly green;
Forth to the wood did merry men go,
To gather in the mistletoe.
Thus opened wide the baron's hall
To vassal, tenant, serf and all;
Power laid his rod of rule aside
And ceremony doffed his pride.
The heir, with roses in his shoes,
That night might village partner choose;
The lord, underogating, share
The vulgar game of "Post and Pair."
All hailed, with uncontrolled delight,
And general voice, the happy night
That to the cottage, as the crown,
Brought tidings of salvation down.

The fire, with well-dried logs supplied,
Went roaring up the chimney wide;
The huge hall-table's oaken face,
Scrubbed till it shone, the day to grace,
Bore then upon its massive board
No mark to part the squire and lord.
Then was brought in the lusty brawn
By old blue-coated serving man;
Then the grim boar's head frowned on high,
Crested with bays and rosemary.
Well can the green-garbed ranger tell
How, when and where the monster fell;
What dogs before his death he tore,
And all the baitings of the boar.

The wassal round, in good brown bowls,
Garnished with ribbons, blithely trowls.
There the huge sirloin reeked: hard by
Plum-porridge stood, and Christmas pye;
Nor failed old Scotland to produce,
At such high-tide, her savory goose.

Then came the merry maskers in,
And carols roared with blithesome din.
If unmelodious was the song,
It was a hearty note, and strong;
Who lists may in their murmuring see
Traces of ancient mystery;
White shirts supplied the masquerade,
And smutted cheeks the visors made;
But O, what maskers richly dight,
Can boast of bosoms half so light!
England was "merry England" when
Old Christmas brought his sports again;
'Twas Christmas broached the mightiest ale,
'Twas Christmas told the merriest tale;
A Christmas gambol oft would cheer
The poor man's heart through half the year.

SLY SANTA CLAUS
MRS. C.S. STONE

All the house was asleep,
And the fire burning low,
When, from far up the chimney,
Came down a "Ho! ho!"
And a little, round man,
With a terrible scratching,
Dropped into the room
With a wink that was catching.
Yes, down he came, bumping,
And thumping, and jumping,
And picking himself up without sign
of a bruise!

"Ho! ho!" he kept on,
As if bursting with cheer.
"Good children, gay children,
Glad children, see here!
I have brought you fine dolls,
And gay trumpets, and rings,
Noah's arks, and bright skates,
And a host of good things!
I have brought a whole sackful,
A packful, a hackful!
Come hither, come hither, come hither
and choose!

"Ho! ho! What is this?
Why, they all are asleep!
But their stockings are up,
And my presents will keep!
So, in with the candies,
The books, and the toys;

All the goodies I have
For the good girls and boys.
I'll ram them, and jam them,
And slam them, and cram them;
All the stockings will hold while the
tired youngsters snooze."

All the while his round shoulders
Kept ducking and ducking;
And his little, fat fingers
Kept tucking and tucking;
Until every stocking
Bulged out, on the wall,
As if it were bursting,
And ready to fall.

And then, all at once,
With a whisk and a whistle,
And twisting himself
Like a tough bit of gristle,
He bounced up again,
Like the down of a thistle,
And nothing was left but the prints of his shoes.

THE WAITS
MARGARET DELAND

At the break of Christmas Day,
Through the frosty starlight ringing,
Faint and sweet and far away,
Comes the sound of children, singing,
Chanting, singing,
"Cease to mourn,
For Christ is born,
Peace and joy to all men bringing!"

Careless that the chill winds blow,
Growing stronger, sweeter, clearer,
Noiseless footfalls in the snow
Bring the happy voices nearer;
Hear them singing,
"Winter's drear,
But Christ is here,
Mirth and gladness with Him bringing!"

"Merry Christmas!" hear them say,
As the East is growing lighter;
"May the joy of Christmas Day
Make your whole year gladder, brighter!"
Join their singing,
"To each home
Our Christ has come,
All Love's treasures with Him bringing!"

THE KNIGHTING OF THE SIRLOIN OF BEEF BY CHARLES THE SECOND
ANON

The Second Charles of England
Rode forth one Christmas tide,
To hunt a gallant stag of ten,
Of Chingford woods the pride.

The winds blew keen, the snow fell fast,
And made for earth a pall,
As tired steeds and wearied men
Returned to Friday Hall.

The blazing logs, piled on the dogs,
Were pleasant to behold!
And grateful was the steaming feast
To hungry men and cold.

With right good-will all took their fill,
And soon each found relief;
Whilst Charles his royal trencher piled
From one huge loin of beef.

Quoth Charles, "Odd's fish! a noble dish!
Ay, noble made by me!
By kingly right, I dub thee knight—
Sir Loin henceforward be!"

And never was a royal jest
Received with such acclaim:
And never knight than good Sir Loin
More worthy of the name.

THE CHRISTMAS GOOSE AT THE CRATCHITS'

CHARLES DICKENS

You might have thought a goose the rarest of all birds; a feathered phenomenon, to which a black swan was a matter of course; and in truth, it was something like it in that house. Mrs. Cratchit made the gravy (ready before-hand in a little saucepan) hissing hot; Master Peter mashed the potatoes with incredible vigor; Miss Belinda sweetened up the apple-sauce; Martha dusted the hot plates; Bob took Tiny Tim beside him in a tiny corner, at the table; the two young Cratchits set chairs for everybody, not forgetting themselves, and mounting guard upon their posts, crammed spoons into their mouths, lest they should shriek for goose before their turn came to be helped. At last the dishes were set on, and grace was said. It was succeeded by a breathless pause, as Mrs. Cratchit, looking slowly all along the carving knife, prepared to plunge it in the breast; but when she did, and when the long-expected gush of stuffing issued forth, one murmur of delight arose all around the board, and even Tiny Tim, excited by the two young Cratchits, beat on the table with the handle of his knife, and feebly cried hurrah!

There never was such a goose. Bob said he didn't believe there ever was such a goose cooked. Its tenderness and flavor, size and cheapness, were the themes of universal admiration. Eked out by the apple-sauce and mashed potatoes, it was a sufficient dinner for the whole family; indeed, as Mrs. Cratchit said with great delight (surveying one small atom of a bone on the dish), they hadn't ate it all at last! Yet every one had had enough, and the youngest Cratchits in particular were steeped in sage and onion to the eye-brows! But now, the plates being changed by Miss Belinda, Mrs. Cratchit left the room alone—too nervous to bear witnesses—to take the pudding up, and bring it in. Suppose it should not be done enough! Suppose it should break in turning out! Suppose somebody should have got over the wall of the backyard, and stolen it, while they were merry with the goose; a supposition at which the two young Cratchits became livid! All sorts of horrors were supposed.

Hallo! A great deal of steam! The pudding was out of the copper. A smell like a washing-day! That was the cloth. A smell like an eating-house and a pastry cook's next door to each other, with a laundress next door to that! That was the pudding. In half a minute Mrs. Cratchit entered, flushed, but smiling proudly, with the pudding like a speckled cannon-ball, so hard and firm, blazing in half of half-a-quartern of ignited brandy, and bedight with Christmas holly stuck into the top.

Oh, a wonderful pudding! Bob Cratchit said, and calmly too, that he regarded it as the greatest success achieved by Mrs. Cratchit since their marriage. Mrs. Cratchit said that now the weight was off her mind, she would confess she had had her doubts about the quantity of flour. Everybody had something to say about it, but nobody said or thought it was at all a small pudding for so large a family. It would have been flat heresy to do so. Any Cratchit would have blushed to hint at such a thing.

At last the dinner was all done, the cloth was cleared, the hearth swept, and the fire made up. The compound in the jug being tasted and considered perfect, apples and oranges were put upon the table, and a shovelful of chestnuts on the fire. Then all the Cratchit family drew round the hearth, in what Bob Cratchit called a circle, meaning half a one; and at Bob Cratchit's elbow stood the family display of glass—two tumblers, and a custard-cup without a handle.

These held the hot stuff from the jug, however, as well as golden goblets would have done; and Bob served it out with beaming looks, while the chestnuts on the fire sputtered and cracked noisily. Then Bob proposed:

"A merry Christmas to us all, my dears. God bless us!"

Which all the family re-echoed.

"God bless us every one!" said Tiny Tim, the last of all.

GOD BLESS US EVERY ONE
JAMES WHITCOMB RILEY
[From "Sketches in Prose."]

"God bless us every one!" prayed Tiny Tim,
Crippled, and dwarfed of body, yet so tall
Of soul, we tiptoe earth to look on him,
High towering over all.

He loved the loveless world, nor dreamed, indeed,
That it, at best, could give to him, the while,
But pitying glances, when his only need
Was but a cheery smile.

And thus he prayed, "God bless us every one!"
Enfolding all the creeds within the span
Of his child-heart; and so, despising none,
Was nearer saint than man.

I like to fancy God, in Paradise,
Lifting a finger o'er the rhythmic swing
Of chiming harp and song, with eager eyes
Turned earthward, listening—

The Anthem stilled—the angels leaning there
Above the golden walls—the morning sun
Of Christmas bursting flower-like with the prayer,
"God bless us Every One!"

BELLS ACROSS THE SNOWS
FRANCES RIDLEY HAVERGAL
O Christmas, merry Christmas!
Is it really come again,
With its memories and greetings,
With its joy and with its pain?
There's a minor in the carol,
And a shadow in the light,
And a spray of cypress twining
With the holly wreath to-night.
And the hush is never broken
By laughter light and low,
As we listen in the starlight
To the "bells across the snow."

O Christmas, merry Christmas!
'Tis not so very long
Since other voices blended
With the carol and the song!
If we could but hear them singing
As they are singing now,
If we could but see the radiance
Of the crown on each dear brow;
There would be no sigh to smother,
No hidden tear to flow,
As we listen in the starlight
To the "bells across the snow."

O Christmas, merry Christmas!
This never more can be;
We cannot bring again the days
Of our unshadowed glee.
But Christmas, happy Christmas,
Sweet herald of good-will,
With holy songs of glory
Brings holy gladness still.

For peace and hope may brighten,
And patient love may glow,
As we listen in the starlight
To the "bells across the snow."

CHRISTMAS BELLS
HENRY WADSWORTH LONGFELLOW
I heard the bells on Christmas Day
Their old, familiar carols play,
And wild and sweet
The words repeat
Of peace on earth, good-will to men!

And thought how, as the day had come,
The belfries of all Christendom
Had rolled along
The unbroken song
Of peace on earth, good-will to men!

Till, ringing, swinging on its way,
The world revolved from night to day
A voice, a chime,
A chant sublime
Of peace on earth, good-will to men!

Then from each black, accursèd mouth
The cannon thundered in the South
And with the sound
The carols drowned
Of peace on earth, good-will to men!

It was as if an earthquake rent
The hearth-stones of a continent,
And made forlorn
The households born
Of peace on earth, good-will to men!

And in despair I bowed my head;
"There is no peace on earth," I said;
"For hate is strong
And mocks the song

Of peace on earth, good-will to men!"

Then pealed the bells more loud and deep.
"God is not dead; nor doth He sleep!
The Wrong shall fail,
The Right prevail,
With peace on earth, good-will to men!"

MINSTRELS AND MAIDS
WILLIAM MORRIS

Outlanders, whence come ye last?
The snow in the street and the wind on the door
Through what green seas and great have ye past?
Minstrels and maids, stand forth on the floor

From far away, O masters mine,
The snow in the street and the wind on the door
We come to bear you goodly wine,
Minstrels and maids, stand forth on the floor

From far away we come to you,
The snow in the street and the wind on the door
To tell of great tidings strange and true,
Minstrels and maids, stand forth on the floor

News, news of the Trinity,
The snow in the street and the wind on the door
And Mary and Joseph from over the sea!
Minstrels and maids, stand forth on the floor

For as we wandered far and wide,
The snow in the street and the wind on the door
What hap do you deem there should us betide!
Minstrels and maids, stand forth on the floor

Under a bent when the night was deep,
The snow in the street and the wind on the door
There lay three shepherds tending their sheep.
Minstrels and maids, stand forth on the floor

"O ye shepherds, what have ye seen,
The snow in the street and the wind on the door
To slay your sorrow, and heal your teen?"
Minstrels and maids, stand forth on the floor

102

"In an ox-stall this night we saw,
The snow in the street and the wind on the door
A babe and a maid without a flaw.
Minstrels and maids, stand forth on the floor

"There was an old man there beside,
The snow in the street and the wind on the door
His hair was white and his hood was wide.
Minstrels and maids, stand forth on the floor

"And as we gazed this thing upon,
The snow in the street and the wind on the door
Those twain knelt down to the Little One,
Minstrels and maids, stand forth on the floor

"And a marvellous song we straight did hear,
The snow in the street and the wind on the door
That slew our sorrow and healed our care."
Minstrels and maids, stand forth on the floor

News of a fair and marvellous thing,
The snow in the street and the wind on the door
Nowell, nowell, nowell, we sing!
Minstrels and maids, stand forth on the floor

INEXHAUSTIBILITY OF THE SUBJECT OF CHRISTMAS
LEIGH HUNT

So many things have been said of late years about Christmas, that it is supposed by some there is no saying more. O they of little faith! What! do they suppose that every thing has been said that *can* be said about any one Christmas thing?

About beef, for instance?

About plum-pudding?

About mince-pie?

About holly?

About ivy?

About rosemary?

About mistletoe? (Good Heavens! what an immense number of things remain to be said about mistletoe!)

About Christmas Eve?

About hunt-the-slipper?

About hot cockles?

About blind-man's-buff?

About shoeing the wild-mare?

About thread-the-needle?

About he-can-do-little-that-can't-do-this?

About puss-in-the-corner?

About snap-dragon?

About forfeits?

About Miss Smith?

About the bell-man?

About the waits?

About chilblains?

About carols?

About the fire?

About the block on it?

About school-boys?

About their mothers?

About Christmas-boxes?

About turkeys?

About Hogmany?

About goose-pie?
About mumming?
About saluting the apple-trees?
About brawn?
About plum-porridge?
About hobby-horse?
About hoppings?
About wakes?
About "feed-the-dove"?
About hackins?
About yule-doughs?
About going-a-gooding?
About loaf-stealing?
About *Julklaps*? (Who has exhausted that subject, we should like to know?)
About wad-shooting?
About elder-wine?
About pantomimes?
About cards?
About New-Year's Day?
About gifts?
About wassail?
About Twelfth-cake?
About king and queen?
About characters?
About eating too much?
About aldermen?
About the doctor?
About all being in the wrong?
About charity?
About all being in the right?
About faith, hope, and endeavor?
About the greatest plum-pudding for the greatest number?
Esto perpetua,—that is, faith, hope and charity, and endeavor; and plum-pudding enough by and by, all the year round, for everybody that likes it. Why that should not be the case, we

cannot see,—seeing that the earth is big, and human kind teachable, and God very good, and inciting us to do it. Meantime, gravity apart, we ask anybody whether any of the above subjects are exhausted; and we inform everybody, that all the above customs still exist in some parts of our beloved country, however unintelligible they may have become in others. But to give a specimen of the non-exhaustion of any one of their topics.

Beef, for example. Now, we should like to know who has exhausted the subject of the fine old roast Christmas piece of beef, from its original appearance in the meadows as part of the noble sultan of the herd, glorious old Taurus,—the lord of the sturdy brow and ponderous agility, a sort of thunderbolt of a beast, well chosen by Jove to disguise in, one of Nature's most striking compounds of apparent heaviness and unencumbered activity,—up to its contribution to the noble Christmas-dinner, smoking from the spit, and flanked by the outposts of Bacchus. John Bull (cannibalism apart) hails it like a sort of relation. He makes it part of his flesh and blood; glories in it; was named after it; has it served up, on solemn occasions, with music and a hymn, as it was the other day at the royal city dinner:—

"Oh the roast beef of old England!
And oh the old English roast beef!"

"*And* oh!" observe, not merely "oh!" again; but "and" with it; as if, though the same piece of beef, it were also another,— another and the same,—cut, and come again; making two of one, in order to express intensity and reduplication of satisfaction:—

"Oh the roast beef of old England!
And oh the old English roast beef!"

We beg to assure the reader, that a whole *Seer* might be written on this single point of the Christmas-dinner; and "shall we be told" (as orators exclaim), "and this, too, in a British land," that the subject is "*exhausted*"!

Then plum-pudding! What a word is that! how plump and plump again! How round and repeated and plenipotential!

106

(There are two p's, observe, in plenipotential; and so there are in plum-pudding. We love an exquisite fitness,—a might and wealth of adaptation). Why, the whole round cheek of universal childhood is in the idea of plum-pudding; ay, and the weight of manhood, and the plenitude of the majesty of city dames. Wealth itself is symbolized by the least of its fruity particles. "A plum" is a city fortune,—a million of money. He (the old boy, who has earned it)—
"Puts in his thumb,
videlicet, into his pocket,
And pulls out a plum,
And says, What a *good man* am I!"
Observe a little boy at a Christmas-dinner, and his grandfather opposite him. What a world of secret similarity there is between them! How hope in one, and retrospection in the other, and appetite in both, meet over the same ground of pudding, and understand it to a nicety! How the senior banters the little boy on his third slice! and how the little boy thinks within himself that he dines that day as well as the senior! How both look hot and red and smiling, and juvenile. How the little boy is conscious of the Christmas-box in his pocket! (of which, indeed, the grandfather jocosely puts him in mind); and how the grandfather is quite as conscious of the plum, or part of a plum, or whatever fraction it may be, in his own! How he incites the little boy to love money and good dinners all his life! and how determined the little boy is to abide by his advice,—with a secret addition in favor of holidays and marbles,—to which there is an analogy, in the senior's mind, on the side of trips to Hastings, and a game at whist! Finally, the old gentleman sees his own face in the pretty smooth one of the child; and if the child is not best pleased at his proclamation of the likeness (in truth, is horrified at it, and thinks it a sort of madness), yet nice observers, who have lived long enough to see the wonderful changes in people's faces from youth to age, probably discern the thing well enough, and feel a movement of pathos at their hearts in considering the world of trouble and emotion that is

the causer of the changes. *That* old man's face was once like that little boy's! *That* little boy's will be one day like that old man's! What a thought to make us all love and respect one another, if not for our fine qualities, let at least for the trouble and sorrow which we all go through!

Ay, and joy too; for all people have their joys as well as troubles, at one time or another,—most likely both together, or in constant alternation: and the greater part of troubles are not the worst things in the world, but only graver forms of the requisite motion of the universe, or workings towards a better condition of things, the greater or less violent according as we give them violence, or respect them like awful but not ill-meaning gods, and entertain them with a rewarded patience. Grave thoughts, you will say, for Christmas. But no season has a greater right to grave thoughts, in passing; and, for that very reason, no season has a greater right to let them pass, and recur to more light ones.

So a noble and merry season to you, my masters; and may we meet, thick and three-fold, many a time and oft, in blithe yet most thoughtful pages! Fail not to call to mind, in the course of the 25th of this month, that the divinest Heart that ever walked the earth was born on that day: and then smile and enjoy yourselves for the rest of it; for mirth is also of Heaven's making, and wondrous was the wine-drinking at Galilee.

SONG OF THE HOLLY
WILLIAM SHAKESPEARE

Blow, blow thou winter wind—
Thou art not so unkind
As man's ingratitude!
Thy tooth is not so keen,
Because thou art not seen,
Although thy breath be rude.
Heigh ho! sing heigh ho! unto the green holly:
Most friendship is feigning, most loving mere folly.
Then heigh ho! the holly!
This life is most jolly!

Freeze, freeze, thou bitter sky—
Thou dost not bite so nigh
As benefits forgot!
Though thou the waters warp,
Thy sting is not so sharp
As friend remembered not.
Heigh ho! sing heigh ho! unto the green holly,
Most friendship is feigning, most loving mere folly.
Then heigh ho, the holly!
This life is most jolly!

UNDER THE HOLLY-BOUGH
CHARLES MACKAY

Ye who have scorned each other,
Or injured friend or brother,
In this fast-fading year;
Ye who, by word or deed,
Have made a kind heart bleed,
Come gather here!
Let sinned against and sinning
Forget their strife's beginning,
And join in friendship now.
Be links no longer broken,
Be sweet forgiveness spoken
Under the Holly-Bough.

Ye who have loved each other,
Sister and friend and brother,
In this fast-fading year:
Mother and sire and child,
Young man and maiden mild,
Come gather here;
And let your heart grow fonder,
As memory shall ponder
Each past unbroken vow;
Old loves and younger wooing
Are sweet in the renewing
Under the Holly-Bough.

Ye who have nourished sadness,
Estranged from hope and gladness
In this fast-fading year;
Ye with o'erburdened mind,
Made aliens from your kind,
Come gather here.
Let not the useless sorrow
Pursue you night and morrow,

If e'er you hoped, hope now.
Take heart,—uncloud your faces,
And join in our embraces
Under the Holly-Bough.

CEREMONIES FOR CHRISTMAS
ROBERT HERRICK

Come, bring with a noise,
My merry, merry boys,
The Christmas log to the firing,
While my good dame, she
Bids ye all be free,
And drink to your heart's desiring.

With the last year's brand
Light the new block, and
For good success in his spending,
On your psalteries play,
That sweet luck may
Come while the log is a-teending.

Drink now the strong beer,
Cut the white loaf here,
The while the meat is a-shredding;
For the rare mince-pie,
And the plums stand by,
To fill the paste that's a kneading.

SANTA CLAUS
ANON

He comes in the night! He comes in the night!
He softly, silently comes;
While the little brown heads on the pillows so white
Are dreaming of bugles and drums.
He cuts through the snow like a ship through the foam,
While the white flakes around him whirl;
Who tells him I know not, but he findeth the home
Of each good little boy and girl.

His sleigh it is long, and deep, and wide;
It will carry a host of things,
While dozens of drums hang over the side,
With the sticks sticking under the strings:
And yet not the sound of a drum is heard,
Not a bugle blast is blown,
As he mounts to the chimney-top like a bird,
And drops to the hearth like a stone.

The little red stockings he silently fills,
Till the stockings will hold no more;
The bright little sleds for the great snow hills
Are quickly set down on the floor.
Then Santa Claus mounts to the roof like a bird,
And glides to his seat in the sleigh;
Not the sound of a bugle or drum is heard
As he noiselessly gallops away.

He rides to the East, and he rides to the West,
Of his goodies he touches not one;
He eateth the crumbs of the Christmas feast
When the dear little folks are done.
Old Santa Claus doeth all that he can;

This beautiful mission is his;
Then, children, be good to the little old man,
When you find who the little man is.

THE CEREMONIES FOR CHRISTMAS DAY
ROBERT HERRICK

Kindle the Christmas brand, and then
Till sunset let it burn;
Which quench'd, then lay it up again
Till Christmas next return.

Part must be kept wherewith to teend
The Christmas log next year,
And where 'tis safely kept, the fiend
Can do no mischief there.

DECEMBER

HARRIET F. BLODGETT

I

Oh! holly branch and mistletoe.
And Christmas chimes where'er we go.
And stockings pinned up in a row!
These are thy gifts, December!

II

And if the year has made thee old,
And silvered all thy locks of gold,
Thy heart has never been a-cold
Or known a fading ember.

III

The whole world is a Christmas tree,
And stars its many candles be.
Oh! sing a carol joyfully
The year's great feast in keeping!

IV

For once, on a December night
An angel held a candle bright.
And led three wise men by its light
To where a child was sleeping.

THE FESTIVAL OF ST. NICHOLAS
MARY MAPES DODGE

We all know how, before the Christmas-tree began to flourish in the home-life of our country, a certain "right jolly old elf," with "eight tiny reindeer," used to drive his sleigh-load of toys up to our housetops, and then bound down the chimney to fill the stockings so hopefully hung by the fireplace. His friends called him Santa Claus; and those who were most intimate ventured to say, "Old Nick." It was said that he originally came from Holland. Doubtless he did; but, if so, he certainly, like many other foreigners, changed his ways very much after landing upon our shores. In Holland, St. Nicholas is a veritable saint, and often appears in full costume, with his embroidered robes glittering with gems and gold, his mitre, his crosier, and his jewelled gloves. *Here* Santa Claus comes rollicking along on the 25th of December, our Holy Christmas morn; but in Holland, St. Nicholas visits earth on the 5th, a time especially appropriated to him. Early on the morning of the 6th, which is St. Nicholas Day, he distributes his candies, toys and treasures, and then vanishes for a year.

Christmas Day is devoted by the Hollanders to church-rites and pleasant family visiting. It is on St. Nicholas Eve that their young people become half wild with joy and expectation. To some of them it is a sorry time; for the saint is very candid, and, if any of them have been bad during the past year, he is quite sure to tell them so. Sometimes he carries a birch-rod under his arm, and advises the parents to give them scoldings in place of confections, and floggings instead of joys.

It was well that the boys hastened to their abodes on that bright winter evening; for, in less than an hour afterwards, the saint made his appearance in half the homes of Holland. He visited the king's palace, and in the self-same moment appeared in Annie Bouman's comfortable home. Probably one of our silver half-dollars would have purchased all that his saintship left at the peasant Bouman's. But a half-dollar's worth will sometimes do for the poor what hundreds of dollars may fail to do for the

116

rich: it makes them happy and grateful, fills them with new peace and love.

Hilda van Gleck's little brothers and sisters were in a high state of excitement that night. They had been admitted into the grand parlor: they were dressed in their best, and had been given two cakes apiece at supper. Hilda was as joyous as any. Why not? St. Nicholas would never cross a girl of fourteen from his list, just because she was tall and looked almost like a woman. On the contrary, he would probably exert himself to do honor to such an august-looking damsel. Who could tell? So she sported and laughed and danced as gayly as the youngest, and was the soul of all their merry games. Father, mother and grandmother looked on approvingly; so did grandfather, before he spread his large red handkerchief over his face, leaving only the top of his skull-cap visible. This kerchief was his ensign of sleep.

Earlier in the evening, all had joined in the fun. In the general hilarity, there had seemed to be a difference only in bulk between grandfather and the baby. Indeed, a shade of solemn expectation, now and then flitting across the faces of the younger members, had made them seem rather more thoughtful than their elders.

Now the spirit of fun reigned supreme. The very flames danced and capered in the polished grate. A pair of prim candles, that had been staring at the astral lamp, began to wink at other candles far away in the mirrors. There was a long bell-rope suspended from the ceiling in the corner, made of glass beads, netted over a cord nearly as thick as your wrist. It generally hung in the shadow, and made no sign; but to-night it twinkled from end to end. Its handle of crimson glass sent reckless dashes of red at the papered wall, turning its dainty blue stripes into purple. Passers-by halted to catch the merry laughter floating through curtain and sash into the street, then skipped on their way with the startled consciousness that the village was wide awake. At last matters grew so uproarious that the grandsire's red kerchief came down from his face with a jerk.

117

What decent old gentleman could sleep in such a racket! Mynheer van Gleck regarded his children with astonishment. The baby even showed symptoms of hysterics. It was high time to attend to business. Mevrouw suggested that, if they wished to see the good St. Nicholas, they should sing the same loving invitation that had brought him the year before.

The baby stared, and thrust his fist into his mouth, as Mynheer put him down upon the floor. Soon he sat erect, and looked with a sweet scowl at the company. With his lace and embroideries, and his crown of blue ribbon and whalebone (for he was not quite past the tumbling age), he looked like the king of babies.

The other children, each holding a pretty willow basket, formed at once in a ring, and moved slowly around the little fellow, lifting their eyes meanwhile; for the saint to whom they were about to address themselves was yet in mysterious quarters. Mevrouw commenced playing softly upon the piano; soon the voices rose,—gentle, youthful voices, rendered all the sweeter for their tremor,—

"Welcome, friend! St. Nicholas, welcome!
Bring no rod for us to-night!
While our voices bid thee welcome,
Every heart with joy is light.

"Tell us every fault and failing;
We will bear thy keenest railing
So we sing, so we sing:
Thou shalt tell us everything!

"Welcome, friend! St. Nicholas, welcome!
Welcome to this merry band!
Happy children greet thee, welcome!
Thou art gladdening all the land.

"Fill each empty hand and basket;
'T is thy little ones who ask it.

118

So we sing, so we sing:
Thou wilt bring us everything!"

During the chorus, sundry glances, half in eagerness, half in dread, had been cast towards the polished folding-doors. Now a loud knocking was heard. The circle was broken in an instant.

Some of the little ones, with a strange mixture of fear and delight, pressed against their mother's knee. Grandfather bent forward, with his chin resting upon his hand; grandmother lifted her spectacles; Mynheer van Gleck, seated by the fireplace, slowly drew his meerschaum from his mouth; while Hilda and the other children settled themselves beside him in an expectant group.

The knocking was heard again.

"Come in," said the mevrouw, softly.

The door slowly opened; and St. Nicholas, in full array, stood before them. You could have heard a pin drop. Soon he spoke. What a mysterious majesty in his voice! what kindliness in his tone!

"Karel van Gleck, I am pleased to greet thee, and thy honored *vrouw*, Kathrine, and thy son, and his good *vrouw*, Annie.

"Children, I greet ye all,—Hendrick, Hilda, Broom, Katy, Huygens and Lucretia. And thy cousins,—Wolfert, Diedrich, Mayken, Voost and Katrina. Good children ye have been, in the main, since I last accosted ye. Diedrich was rude at the Haarlem fair last fall; but he has tried to atone for it since. Mayken has failed, of late, in her lessons; and too many sweets and trifles have gone to her lips, and too few stivers to her charity-box. Diedrich, I trust, will be a polite, manly boy for the future; and Mayken will endeavor to shine as a student. Let her remember, too, that economy and thrift are needed in the foundation of a worthy and generous life. Little Katy has been cruel to the cat more than once. St. Nicholas can hear the cat cry when its tail is pulled. I will forgive her, if she will remember from this hour that the smallest dumb creatures have feeling, and must not be abused."

As Katy burst into a frightened cry, the saint graciously remained silent until she was soothed.

"Master Broom," he resumed, "I warn thee that boys who are in the habit of putting snuff upon the foot-stove of the school-mistress may one day be discovered, and receive a flogging—" (Master Broom colored, and stared in great astonishment.) "But, thou art such an excellent scholar, I shall make thee no further reproof.

"Thou, Hendrick, didst distinguish thyself in the archery match last spring, and hit the *doel*,[A] though the bird was swung before it to unsteady thine eye. I give thee credit for excelling in manly sport and exercise; though I must not unduly countenance thy boat-racing, since it leaves thee too little time for thy proper studies.

[A]Bull's-eye.

"Lucretia and Hilda shall have a blessed sleep to-night. The consciousness of kindness to the poor, devotion in their souls, and cheerful, hearty obedience to household rule, will render them happy.

"With one and all I avow myself well content. Goodness, industry, benevolence and thrift have prevailed in your midst. Therefore, my blessing upon you; and may the New Year find all treading the paths of obedience, wisdom and love! To-morrow you shall find more substantial proofs that I have been in your home. Farewell!"

With these words came a great shower of sugar-plums upon a linen sheet spread out in front of the doors. A general scramble followed. The children fairly tumbled over each other in their eagerness to fill their baskets. Mevrouw cautiously held the baby down upon the sheet till the chubby little fists were filled. Then the bravest of the youngsters sprang up and threw open the closed doors. In vain they searched the mysterious apartment. St. Nicholas was nowhere to be seen.

Soon they all sped to another room, where stood a table, covered with the whitest of linen damask. Each child, in a flutter of pleasure, laid a shoe upon it, and each shoe held a little hay

120

for the good saint's horse. The door was then carefully locked, and its key hidden in the mother's bedroom. Next followed good-night kisses, a grand family procession to the upper floor, merry farewells at bedroom doors, and silence, at last, reigned in the Van Gleck mansion.

Early the next morning, the door was solemnly unlocked and opened in the presence of the assembled household; when, lo! a sight appeared, proving good St. Nicholas to be a saint of his word.

Every shoe was filled to overflowing; and beside each stood a many-colored pile. The table was heavy with its load of presents,—candies, toys, trinkets, books and other articles. Every one had gifts, from grandfather down to the baby.

THE CHRISTMAS HOLLY
ELIZA COOK

The holly! the holly! oh, twine it with bay—
Come give the holly a song;
For it helps to drive stern winter away,
With his garment so sombre and long;

It peeps through the trees with its berries of red,
And its leaves of burnished green,
When the flowers and fruits have long been dead,
And not even the daisy is seen.
Then sing to the holly, the Christmas holly,
That hangs over peasant and king;
While we laugh and carouse 'neath its glittering boughs,
To the Christmas holly we'll sing.

The gale may whistle, the frost may come
To fetter the gurgling rill;
The woods may be bare, and warblers dumb,
But holly is beautiful still.
In the revel and light of princely halls
The bright holly branch is found;
And its shadow falls on the lowliest walls,
While the brimming horn goes round.

The ivy lives long, but its home must be
Where graves and ruins are spread;
There's beauty about the cypress tree,
But it flourishes near the dead;
The laurel the warrior's brow may wreathe,
But it tells of tears and blood;
I sing the holly, and who can breathe
Aught of that that is not good?

Then sing to the holly, the Christmas holly,
That hangs over peasant and king;

While we laugh and carouse 'neath its glittering boughs,
To the Christmas holly we'll sing.

TO THE FIR-TREE
FROM THE GERMAN

O Fir-tree green! O Fir-tree green!
Your leaves are constant ever,
Not only in the summer time,
But through the winter's snow and rime
You're fresh and green forever.

O Fir-tree green! O Fir-tree green!
I still shall love you dearly!
How oft to me on Christmas night
Your laden boughs have brought delight.
O Fir-tree green! O Fir-tree green!
I still shall love you dearly.

THE MAHOGANY-TREE
WILLIAM MAKEPEACE THACKERAY

Christmas is here;
Winds whistle shrill,
Icy and chill,
Little care we;
Little we fear
Weather without,
Sheltered about
The Mahogany-Tree.

Once on the boughs
Birds of rare plume
Sang in its bloom;
Night-birds are we;
Here we carouse,
Singing, like them,
Perched round the stem
Of the jolly old tree.

Here let us sport,
Boys, as we sit—
Laughter and wit
Flashing so free.
Life is but short—
When we are gone,
Let them sing on,
Round the old tree.

Evenings we knew,
Happy as this;
Faces we miss,
Pleasant to see.
Kind hearts and true,
Gentle and just,
Peace to your dust!

We sing round the tree.

Care like a dun,
Lurks at the gate;
Let the dog wait;
Happy we'll be!
Drink, every one;
Pile up the coals;
Fill the red bowls,
Round the old tree!

Drain we the cup.—
Friend, art afraid?
Spirits are laid
In the Red Sea.
Mantle it up;
Empty it yet;
Let us forget,
Round the old tree!

Sorrows begone!
Life and its ills,
Duns and their bills,
Bid we to flee.
Come with the dawn,
Blue-devil sprite;
Leave us to-night,
Round the old tree!

CHRISTMAS
WASHINGTON IRVING

But is old, old, good old Christmas gone? Nothing but the hair
on
his good, gray, old head and beard left? Well, I will have that,
seeing I cannot have more of him.
Hue and Cry after Christmas.

A man might then behold
At Christmas, in each hall,
Good fires to curb the cold,
And meat for great and small.
The neighbors were friendly bidden,
And all had welcome true,
The poor from the gates were not chidden,
When this old cap was new.
Old Song.

There is nothing in England that exercises a more delightful spell
over my imagination than the lingerings of the holiday customs
and rural games of former times. They recall the pictures my
fancy used to draw in the May morning of life, when as yet I
only knew the world through books, and believed it to be all
that poets had painted it; and they bring with them the flavor of
those honest days of yore, in which, perhaps with equal fallacy,
I am apt to think the world was more homebred, social, and
joyous than at present. I regret to say that they are daily
growing more and more faint, being gradually worn away by
time, but still more obliterated by modern fashion. They
resemble those picturesque morsels of Gothic architecture,
which we see crumbling in various parts of the country, partly
dilapidated by the waste of ages, and partly lost in the additions
and alterations of latter days. Poetry, however, clings with
cherishing fondness about the rural game and holiday revel,
from which it has derived so many of its themes—as the ivy
winds its rich foliage about the Gothic arch and mouldering
tower, gratefully repaying their support, by clasping together

their tottering remains, and, as it were, embalming them in verdure.

Of all the old festivals, however, that of Christmas awakens the strongest and most heartfelt associations. There is a tone of solemn and sacred feeling that blends with our conviviality, and lifts the spirit to a state of hallowed and elevated enjoyment. The services of the church about this season are extremely tender and inspiring: they dwell on the beautiful story of the origin of our faith, and the pastoral scenes that accompanied its announcement; they gradually increase in fervor and pathos during the season of Advent, until they break forth in full jubilee on the morning that brought peace and good-will to men. I do not know a grander effect of music on the moral feelings than to hear the full choir and the pealing organ performing a Christmas anthem in a cathedral, and filling every part of the vast pile with triumphant harmony.

It is a beautiful arrangement, also, derived from the days of yore, that this festival, which commemorates the announcement of the religion of peace and love, has been made the season for gathering together of family connections, and drawing closer again those bands of kindred hearts, which the cares and pleasures and sorrows of the world are continually operating to cast loose; of calling back the children of a family, who have launched forth in life, and wandered widely asunder, once more to assemble about the paternal hearth, that rallying-place of the affections, there to grow young and loving again among the endearing mementos of childhood.

There is something in the very season of the year, that gives a charm to the festivity of Christmas. At other times, we derive a great portion of our pleasures from the mere beauties of Nature. Our feelings sally forth and dissipate themselves over the sunny landscape, and we "live abroad and everywhere." The song of the bird, the murmur of the stream, the breathing fragrance of spring, the soft voluptuousness of summer, the golden pomp of autumn; earth with its mantle of refreshing green, and heaven with its deep, delicious blue and its cloudy

128

magnificence,—all fill us with mute but exquisite delight, and we revel in the luxury of mere sensation. But in the depth of winter, when Nature lies despoiled of every charm, and wrapped in her shroud of sheeted snow, we turn for our gratifications to moral sources. The dreariness and desolation of our landscape, the short gloomy days and darksome nights, while they circumscribe our wanderings, shut in our feelings also from rambling abroad, and make us more keenly disposed for the pleasures of the social circle. Our thoughts are more concentrated; our friendly sympathies more aroused. We feel more sensibly the charm of each other's society, and are brought more closely together by dependence on each other for enjoyment. Heart calleth unto heart, and we draw our pleasures from the deep wells of living kindness which lie in the quiet recesses of our bosoms; and which, when resorted to, furnish forth the pure element of domestic felicity.

The pitchy gloom without makes the heart dilate on entering the room filled with the glow and warmth of the evening fire. The ruddy blaze diffuses an artificial summer and sunshine through the room, and lights up each countenance with a kindlier welcome. Where does the honest face of hospitality expand into a broader and more cordial smile—where is the shy glance of love more sweetly eloquent—than by the winter fireside? and as the hollow blast of wintry wind rushes through the hall, claps the distant door, whistles about the casement, and rumbles down the chimney, what can be more grateful than that feeling of sober and sheltered security, with which we look around upon the comfortable chamber, and the scene of domestic hilarity?

The English, from the great prevalence of rural habits throughout every class of society, have always been fond of those festivals and holidays which agreeably interrupt the stillness of country life; and they were in former days particularly observant of the religious and social rights of Christmas. It is inspiring to read even the dry details which some antiquaries have given of the quaint humors, the burlesque

129

pageants, the complete abandonment to mirth and good fellowship, with which this festival was celebrated. It seemed to throw open every door, unlock every heart. It brought the peasant and the peer together, and blended all ranks in one warm generous flow of joy and kindness. The old halls of castles and manor-houses resounded with the harp and the Christmas carol, and their ample boards groaned under the weight of hospitality. Even the poorest cottage welcomed the festive season with green decorations of bay and holly—the cheerful fire glanced its rays through the lattice, inviting the passenger to raise the latch, and join the gossip knot huddled round the hearth beguiling the long evening with legendary jokes, and oft-told Christmas tales.

One of the least pleasing effects of modern refinement is the havoc it has made among the hearty old holiday customs. It has completely taken off the sharp touchings and spirited reliefs of these embellishments of life, and has worn down society into a more smooth and polished, but certainly a less characteristic surface. Many of the games and ceremonials of Christmas have entirely disappeared, and, like the sherris sack of old Falstaff, are become matters of speculation and dispute among commentators. They flourished in times full of spirit and lustihood, when men enjoyed life roughly, but heartily and vigorously: times wild and picturesque, which have furnished poetry with its richest materials, and the drama with its most attractive variety of characters and manners. The world has become more worldly. There is more of dissipation and less enjoyment. Pleasure has expanded into a broader, but a shallower stream, and has forsaken many of those deep and quiet channels, where it flowed sweetly through the calm bosom of domestic life. Society has acquired a more enlightened and elegant tone; but it has lost many of its strong local peculiarities, its homebred feelings, its honest fireside delights. The traditionary customs of golden-hearted antiquity, its feudal hospitalities, and lordly wassailings, have passed away with the baronial castles and stately manor-houses in which they were celebrated. They comported with the shadowy hall, the great oaken gallery, and the tapestried parlor, but are unfitted for the light showy saloons and gay drawing-rooms of the modern villa.

Shorn, however, as it is, of its ancient and festive honors, Christmas is still a period of delightful excitement in England. It is gratifying to see that home feeling completely aroused which holds so powerful a place in every English bosom. The preparations making on every side for the social board that is again to unite friends and kindred—the presents of good cheer passing and repassing, those tokens of regard and quickeners of kind feelings—the evergreens distributed about houses and churches, emblems of peace and gladness—all these have the most pleasing effect in producing fond associations, and kindling benevolent sympathies. Even the sound of the waits, rude as may be their minstrelsy, breaks upon the midwatches of a winter night with the effect of perfect harmony. As I have been awakened by them in that still and solemn hour "when deep sleep falleth upon man," I have listened with a hushed delight, and connecting them with the sacred and joyous occasion, have almost fancied them into another celestial choir, announcing peace and good-will to mankind. How delightfully the imagination, when wrought upon by these moral influences, turns everything to melody and beauty! The very crowing of the cock, heard sometimes in the profound repose of the country, "telling the night-watches to his feathery dames," was thought by the common people to announce the approach of the sacred festival:

"Some say that ever 'gainst that season comes
Wherein our Saviour's birth was celebrated,
This bird of dawning singeth all night long:
And then, they say, no spirit dares stir abroad;
The nights are wholesome—then no planets strike,
No fairy takes, no witch hath power to charm,
So hallowed and so gracious is the time."

131

Amidst the general call to happiness, the bustle of the spirits, and stir of the affections, which prevail at this period, what bosom can remain insensible? It is, indeed, the season of regenerated feeling—the season for kindling not merely the fire of hospitality in the hall, but the genial flame of charity in the heart. The scene of early love again rises green to memory beyond the sterile waste of years, and the idea of home, fraught with the fragrance of home-dwelling joys, reanimates the drooping spirit—as the Arabian breeze will sometimes waft the freshness of the distant fields to the weary pilgrim of the desert. Stranger and sojourner as I am in the land—though for me no social hearth may blaze, no hospitable roof throw open its doors, nor the warm grasp of friendship welcome me at the threshold—yet I feel the influence of the season beaming into my soul from the happy looks of those around me. Surely happiness is reflective, like the light of heaven; and every countenance bright with smiles, and glowing with innocent enjoyment, is a mirror transmitting to others the rays of a supreme and ever-shining benevolence. He who can turn churlishly away from contemplating the felicity of his fellow-beings, and can sit down darkling and repining in his loneliness when all around is joyful, may have his moments of strong excitement and selfish gratification, but he wants the genial and social sympathies which constitute the charm of a merry Christmas.

CHURCH DECKING AT CHRISTMAS
WILLIAM WORDSWORTH

Would that our scrupulous sires had dared to leave
Less scanty measure of those graceful rites
And usages, whose due return invites
A stir of mind too natural to deceive;
Giving the memory help when she could weave
A crown for Hope!—I dread the boasted lights
That all too often are but fiery blights,
Killing the bud o'er which in vain we grieve.
Go, seek, when Christmas snows discomfort bring,
The counter Spirit found in some gay church
Green with fresh holly, every pew a perch
In which the linnet or the thrush might sing,
Merry and loud, and safe from prying search,
Strains offered only to the genial spring.

SO, NOW IS COME OUR JOYFULST FEAST
GEORGE WITHER

So, now is come our joyfulst feast,
Let every man be jolly;
Each room with ivy leaves is drest,
And every post with holly.
Though some churls at our mirth repine,
Round your foreheads garlands twine;
Drown sorrow in a cup of wine,
And let us all be merry.

Now all our neighbours' chimnies smoke,
And Christmas logs are burning;
Their ovens they with baked meats choke,
And all their spits are turning.
Without the door let sorrow lie;
And if for cold it hap to die,
We'll bury't in a Christmas pie,
And evermore be merry.

Now every lad is wondrous trim,
And no man minds his labour;
Our lasses have provided them
A bag-pipe and a tabor;
Young men and maids, and girls and boys,
Give life to one another's joys;
And you anon shall by their noise
Perceive that they are merry.

Rank misers now do sparing shun;
Their hall of music soundeth;
And dogs thence with whole shoulders run,
So all things there aboundeth.
The country folks themselves advance
For crowdy-mutton's[A] come out of France;

And Jack shall pipe, and Jill shall dance,
And all the town be merry.
[A]Fiddlers.

FAIRY FACES

ANON

Out of the mists of childhood,
Steeped in a golden glory,
Come dreamy forms and faces,
Snatches of song and story;
Whispers of sweet, still faces;
Rays of ethereal glimmer,
That gleam like sunny heavens,
Ne'er to grow colder or dimmer:
Now far in the distance, now shining near,
Lighting the snows of the shivering year.

Faces there are that tremble,
Bleared with a silent weeping,
Weird in a shadowy sorrow,
As if endless vigil keeping.
Faces of dazzling brightness,
With childlike radiance lighted,
Flashing with many a beauty,
Nor care nor time had blighted.
But o'er them all there's a glamour thrown.
Bright with the dreamy distance alone.

Aglow in the Christmas halo,
Shining with heavenly lustre,
These are the fairy faces
That round the hearthstone cluster.
These the deep, tender records,
Sacred in all their meetness,
That, wakening purest fancies,
Soften us with their sweetness;
As, gathered where flickering fagots burn,
We welcome the holy season's return.

MERRY CHRISTMAS

ANON

In the rush of the merry morning,
When the red burns through the gray,
And the wintry world lies waiting
For the glory of the day;
Then we hear a fitful rushing
Just without upon the stair,
See two white phantoms coming,
Catch the gleam of sunny hair.

Are they Christmas fairies stealing
Rows of little socks to fill?
Are they angels floating hither
With their message of good-will?
What sweet spell are these elves weaving,
As like larks they chirp and sing?
Are these palms of peace from heaven
That these lovely spirits bring?

Rosy feet upon the threshold,
Eager faces peeping through,
With the first red ray of sunshine,
Chanting cherubs come in view;
Mistletoe and gleaming holly,
Symbols of a blessed day,
In their chubby hands they carry,
Streaming all along the way.

Well we know them, never weary
Of this innocent surprise;
Waiting, watching, listening always
With full hearts and tender eyes,
While our little household angels,
White and golden in the sun,
Greet us with the sweet old welcome,—
"Merry Christmas, every one!"

A MERRY CHRISTMAS TO YOU
THEODORE LEDYARD CUYLER

My own boyhood was spent in a delightful home on one of the most beautiful farms in Western New York—an experience that any city-bred boy might envy. We had no religious festivals except Thanksgiving Day and Christmas, and the latter was especially welcome, not only on account of the good fare but its good gifts. Christmas was sacred to Santa Claus, the patron saint of good boys and girls. We counted the days until its arrival. If the night before the longed-for festival was one of eager expectation in all our houses, it was a sad time in all barn-yards and turkey-coops and chicken-roosts; for the slaughter was terrible, and the cry of the feathered tribes was like "the mourning of Hadadrimmon." As to our experiences within doors, they are portrayed in Dr. Clement C. Moore's immortal lines, "The Night Before Christmas," which is probably the most popular poem for children ever penned in America. As the visits of Santa Claus in the night could only be through the chimney, we hung our stockings where they would be in full sight. Three score and ten years ago such modern contrivances as steam pipes, and those unpoetical holes in the floor called "hot-air registers," were as entirely unknown in our rural regions as gas-burners or telephones. We had a genuine fire-place in our kitchen, big enough to contain an enormous back-log, and broad enough for eight or ten people to form "a circle wide" before it and enjoy the genial warmth.

The last process before going to bed was to suspend our stockings in the chimney jambs; and then we dreamed of Santa Claus, or if we awoke in the night, we listened for the jingling of his sleigh-bells. At the peep of day we were aroused by the voice of my good grandfather, who planted himself in the stairway and shouted in a stentorian tone, "I wish you all a Merry Christmas!" The contest was as to who should give the salutation first, and the old gentleman determined to get the start of us by sounding his greeting to the family before we were out of our rooms. Then came a race for the chimney corner; all the stockings came down quicker than they had gone up. What could not be contained in them was disposed upon the mantelpiece, or elsewhere. I remember that I once received an autograph letter from Santa Claus, full of good counsels; and our colored cook told me that she awoke in the night and, peeping into the kitchen, actually saw the veritable old visitor light a candle and sit down at the table and write it! I believed it all as implicitly as I believed the Ten Commandments, or the story of David and Goliath. Happy days of childish credulity, when fact and fiction were swallowed alike without a misgiving! During my long life I have seen many a day-dream and many an air-castle go the way of Santa Claus and the wonderful "Lamp of Aladdin."

In after years, when I became a parent, my beloved wife and I, determined to make the Christmastide one of the golden days of the twelve months. In mid-winter, when all outside vegetation was bleak and bare, the Christmas-tree in our parlor bloomed in many-colored beauty and bounty. When the tiny candles were all lighted the children and our domestics gathered round it and one of the youngsters rehearsed some pretty juvenile effusion; as "they that had found great spoil." After the happy harvesting of the magic tree in my own home, it was my custom to spend the afternoon or evening in some mission-school and to watch the sparkling eyes of several hundreds of children while a huge Christmas-tree shed down its bounties. Fifty years ago, when the degradation and miseries of the "Five-Points" were first invaded by pioneer philanthropy, it was a thrilling sight to behold the denizens of the slums and their children as they flocked into Mr. Pease's new "House of Industry" and the "Brewery Mission" building. The angelic host over the hills of Bethlehem did not make a more welcome revelation to them "who had sat in darkness and the shadow of death." In these days the squalid regions of our great cities are being explored and improved by various methods of systematic beneficence. "Christian Settlements" are established; Bureaus of Charity are formed and Associations for the relief of the poor are organized. A noble work; but, after all, the most effective "bureau" is one that, in a water-proof and a stout pair of shoes, sallies off on a wintry night to some abode of poverty with not only supplies for suffering bodies, but kind words of sympathy for lonesome hearts. A dollar from a warm hand with a warm word is worth two dollars sent by mail or by a messenger-boy.

The secret of power in doing good is *personal contact*. Our incarnate "Elder Brother" went in person to the sick chamber. He anointed with His own hand the eyes of the blind man and He touched the loathsome leper into health. The portentous chasm between wealth and poverty must be bridged by a span of personal kindness over which the footsteps must turn in only one direction. The personal contact of self sacrificing benevolence with darkness, filth and misery—that is the only remedy. Heart must touch heart. Benevolence also cannot be confined to calendars. Those good people will exhibit the most of the spirit of our Blessed Master who practice Christmas-giving and cheerful, unselfish and zealous Christmas-living through all the circling year.

CHRISTMAS BELLS
ANON
There are sounds in the sky when the year grows old,
And the winds of the winter blow—
When night and the moon are clear and cold,
And the stars shine on the snow,
Or wild is the blast and the bitter sleet
That beats on the window-pane;
But blest on the frosty hills are the feet
Of the Christmas time again!
Chiming sweet when the night wind swells,
Blest is the sound of the Christmas Bells!

Dear are the sounds of the Christmas chimes
In the land of the ivied towers,

And they welcome the dearest of festival times
In this Western world of ours!
Bright on the holly and mistletoe bough
The English firelight falls,
And bright are the wreathed evergreens now
That gladden our own home walls!
And hark! the first sweet note that tells,
The welcome of the Christmas Bells!

The owl that sits in the ivy's shade,
Remote from the ruined tower,
Shall start from his drowsy watch afraid
When the clock shall strike the hour;
And over the fields in their frosty rhyme
The cheery sounds shall go,
And chime shall answer unto chime
Across the moonlit snow!
How sweet the lingering music dwells,—
The music of the Christmas Bells.

It fell not thus in the East afar
Where the Babe in the manger lay;
The wise men followed their guiding star
To the dawn of a milder day;
And the fig and the sycamore gathered green,
And the palm-tree of Deborah rose;
'Twas the strange first Christmas the world had seen—
And it came not in storm and snows.
Not yet on Nazareth's hills and dells
Had floated the sound of Christmas Bells.

The cedars of Lebanon shook in the blast
Of their own cold mountain air;
But nought o'er the wintry plain had passed
To tell that the Lord was there!
The oak and the olive and almond were still,

In the night now worn and thin;
No wind of the winter-time roared from the hill
To waken the guests at the inn;
No dream to them the music tells
That is to come from the Christmas Bells!

The years that have fled like the leaves on the gale
Since the morn of the Miracle-Birth,
Have widened the fame of the marvellous tale
Till the tidings have filled the earth!
And so in the climes of the icy North,
And the lands of the cane and the palm,
By the Alpine cotter's blazing hearth,
And in tropic belts of calm,
Men list to-night the welcome swells,
Sweet and clear, of Christmas Bells!

They are ringing to-night through the Norway firs,
And across the Swedish fells,
And the Cuban palm-tree dreamily stirs
To the sound of those Christmas Bells!
They ring where the Indian Ganges rolls
Its flood through the rice-fields wide;
They swell the far hymns of the Lapps and Poles
To the praise of the Crucified.
Sweeter than tones of the ocean's shells
Mingle the chimes of the Christmas Bells!

The years come not back that have circled away
With the past of the Eastern land,
When He plucked the corn on the Sabbath day
And healed the withered hand:
But the bells shall join in a joyous chime
For the One who walked the sea,
And ring again for the better time
Of the Christ that is to be!

Then ring!—for earth's best promise dwells
In ye, O joyous Prophet Bells!

Ring out at the meeting of night and morn
For the dawn of a happier day!
Lo, the stone from our faith's great sepulchre torn
The angels have rolled away!
And they come to us here in our low abode,
With words like the sunrise gleam,—
Come down and ascend by that heavenly road
That Jacob saw in his dream.
Spirit of love, that in music dwells,
Open our hearts with the Christmas Bells!

Help us to see that the glad heart prays
As well as the bended knees;
That there are in our own as in ancient days
The Scribes and the Pharisees;
That the Mount of Transfiguration still
Looks down on these Christian lands,
And the glorified ones from that holy hill
Are reaching their helping hands.
These be the words our music tells
Of solemn joy, O Christmas Bells!

THE BIRTH OF CHRIST
ALFRED TENNYSON

The time draws near the birth of Christ;
The moon is hid—the night is still;
The Christmas bells from hill to hill
Answer each other in the mist.

Four voices of four hamlets round,
From far and near, on mead and moor,
Swell out and fail, as if a door
Were shut between me and the sound.

Each voice four changes on the wind,
That now dilate and now decrease,
Peace and good-will, good-will and peace,
Peace and good-will to all mankind.

Rise, happy morn! rise, holy morn!
Draw forth the cheerful day from night;
O Father! touch the east, and light
The light that shone when hope was born!

THE CHRISTMAS CAROL
WILLIAM WORDSWORTH

The minstrels played their Christmas tune
To-night beneath my cottage eaves;
While, smitten by a lofty moon,
The encircling laurels, thick with leaves,
Gave back a rich and dazzling sheen
That overpowered their natural green.

Through hill and valley every breeze
Had sunk to rest, with folded wings:
Keen was the air, but could not freeze
Nor check the music of the strings;
So stout and hardy were the band
That scraped the chords with strenuous hand!

And who but listened—till was paid
Respect to every inmate's claim:
The greeting given, the music played,
In honor of each household name,
Duly pronounced with lusty call,
And "Merry Christmas" wished to all!

How touching, when, at midnight, sweep
Snow-muffled winds, and all is dark,

144

To hear, and sink again to sleep!
Or, at an earlier call, to mark
By blazing fire, the still suspense
Of self-complacent innocence;

The mutual nod,—the grave disguise
Of hearts with gladness brimming o'er;
And some unbidden tears that rise
For names once heard, and heard no more;
Tears brightened by the serenade
For infant in the cradle laid.

Hail ancient Manners! sure defence,
Where they survive, of wholesome laws;
Remnants of love whose modest sense
Thus into narrow room withdraws;
Hail, Usages of pristine mould,
And ye that guard them, Mountains old!

CHRISTMAS AT FEZZIWIG'S WAREHOUSE
CHARLES DICKENS

"Yo ho! my boys," said Fezziwig. "No more work to-night;
Christmas Eve, Dick! Christmas, Ebenezer! Let's have the
shutters up," cried old Fezziwig with a sharp clap of his hands,
"before a man can say Jack Robinson...."
"Hilli-ho!" cried old Fezziwig, skipping down from the high desk
with wonderful agility. "Clear away, my lads, and let's have lots
of room here! Hilli-ho, Dick! Cheer up, Ebenezer!"
Clear away! There was nothing they wouldn't have cleared
away, or couldn't have cleared away, with old Fezziwig looking
on. It was done in a minute. Every movable was packed off, as if
it were dismissed from public life forevermore; the floor was
swept and watered, the lamps were trimmed, fuel was heaped
upon the fire; and the warehouse was as snug, and warm, and
dry, and bright a ball-room as you would desire to see upon a
winter's night.

In came a fiddler with a music-book, and went up to the lofty desk and made an orchestra of it and tuned like fifty stomach-aches. In came Mrs. Fezziwig, one vast, substantial smile. In came the three Misses Fezziwig, beaming and lovable. In came the six followers whose hearts they broke. In came all the young men and women employed in the business In came the housemaid with her cousin the baker. In came the cook with her brother's particular friend the milkman. In came the boy from over the way, who was suspected of not having board enough from his master, trying to hide himself behind the girl from next door but one who was proved to have had her ears pulled by her mistress; in they all came, anyhow and everyhow. Away they all went, twenty couple at once; hands half round and back again the other way; down the middle and up again; round and round in various stages of affectionate grouping, old top couple always turning up in the wrong place; new top couple starting off again, as soon as they got there; all top couples at last, and not a bottom one to help them.

When this result was brought about the fiddler struck up "Sir Roger de Coverley." Then old Fezziwig stood out to dance with Mrs. Fezziwig. Top couple, too, with a good stiff piece of work cut out for them; three or four and twenty pairs of partners; people who were not to be trifled with; people who would dance and had no notion of walking.

But if they had been thrice as many—Oh, four times as many— old Fezziwig would have been a match for them, and so would Mrs. Fezziwig. As to her, she was worthy to be his partner in every sense of the term. If that's not high praise, tell me higher and I'll use it. A positive light appeared to issue from Fezziwig's calves. They shone in every part of the dance like moons. You couldn't have predicted at any given time what would become of them next. And when old Fezziwig and Mrs. Fezziwig had gone all through the dance; advance and retire; both hands to your partner, bow and courtesy, corkscrew, thread the needle, and back again to your place; Fezziwig "cut"—cut so deftly that he appeared to wink with his legs, and came upon his feet again without a stagger.

When the clock struck eleven the domestic ball broke up. Mr. and Mrs. Fezziwig took their stations, one on either side of the door, and shaking hands with every person individually, as he or she went out, wished him or her a Merry Christmas!

CHRISTMAS BELLS
JOHN KEBLE

Wake me to-night, my mother dear,
That I may hear
The Christmas Bells, so soft and clear,
To high and low glad tidings tell,
How God the Father loved us well;
How God the Eternal Son
Came to undo what we had done.

SIGNIFICANCE AND SPIRIT

A CHRISTMAS CARMEN
JOHN G. WHITTIER

I

Sound over all waters, reach out from all lands,
The chorus of voices, the clasping of hands;
Sing hymns that were sung by the stars of the morn,
Sing songs of the angels when Jesus was born!
With glad jubilations
Bring hope to the nations!
The dark night is ending and dawn has begun:
Rise, hope of the ages, arise like the sun,
All speech flow to music, all hearts beat as one!

II

Sing the bridal of nations! with chorals of love
Sing out the war-vulture and sing in the dove,
Till the hearts of the peoples keep time in accord
And the voice of the world is the voice of the Lord!
Clasp hands of the nations
In strong gratulations:
The dark night is ending and dawn has begun;
Rise, hope of the ages, arise like the sun,
All speech flow to music, all hearts beat as one!

III

Blow, bugles of battle, the marches of peace;
East, west, north, and south let the long quarrel cease:
Sing the song of great joy that the angels began,
Sing of glory to God and of good-will to man!
Hark! joining in chorus
The heavens bend o'er us!
The dark night is ending and dawn has begun;

148

Rise, hope of the ages, arise like the sun,
All speech flow to music, all hearts beat as one!

THE SPIRIT OF CHRISTMAS
From "Pickwick Papers."
CHARLES DICKENS

And numerous indeed are the hearts to which Christmas brings a brief season of happiness and enjoyment. How many families whose members have been dispersed and scattered far and wide, in the restless struggles of life, are then re-united, and meet once again in that happy state of companionship and mutual good-will, which is a source of such pure and unalloyed delight, and one so incompatible with the cares and sorrows of the world, that the religious belief of the most civilized nations, and the rude traditions of the roughest savages, alike number it among the first joys of a future state of existence, provided for the blest and happy! How many old recollections, and how many dormant sympathies, does Christmas time awaken! We write these words now, many miles distant from the spot at which, year after year, we met on that day, a merry and joyous circle. Many of the hearts that throb so gaily then, have ceased to beat; many of the looks that shone so brightly then, have ceased to glow; the hands we grasped, have grown cold; the eyes we sought, have hid their lustre in the grave; and yet the old house, the room, the merry voices and smiling faces, the jest, the laugh, the most minute and trivial circumstance connected with those happy meetings, crowd upon our mind at each recurrence of the season, as if the last assemblage had been but yesterday. Happy, happy Christmas, that can win us back to the delusions of our childish days, that can recall to the old man the pleasures of his youth, and transport the sailor and the traveller, thousands of miles away, back to his own fireside and his quiet home!

ON GOOD WISHES AT CHRISTMAS
FRISWELL

At Christmas, which is a good holiday for most of us, but especially for that larger and better half of us, the young, there is, as everybody knows, a profusion of good things. The final cause of a great many existences is Christmas Day. How many of that vast flock of geese, which are now peacefully feeding over the long, cold wolds of Norfolk, or are driven gabbling and hissing by the gozzard to their pasture—how many of those very geese were called into being simply for Christmas Day! In the towns, with close streets and fetid courts, where the flaring gas at the corner of an alley marks the only bright spot, a gin-palace, there a goose-club is held; and there, for a short time, is the resting-place, side by side with a bottle of gin, of one of those wise-looking and self-concentrated gobblers, whose name men have generally, and, as we think, unjustly, applied to the silly one amongst themselves.

But it is only the profusion of good things, of cakes, puddings, spices, oranges, and fruits, from sunny Italy and Spain, from India and from Asia, from America, North and South, and even from distant Australia; it is not that amongst us, as long ago with the *Franklin* in Chaucer, that at this time—

"It snowës in our house
Of meate and drinke;"

it is not that we have huge loads of beef chines, ribs, sirloins, legs, necks, breasts, and shoulders of mutton, fillets of veal, whole hogs, and pigs in various stages, from the tender suckling to the stiff-jointed father of a family, whose "back hair" makes good clothes-brushes, and whose head is brought in at college feasts; it is not that the air gives up its choicest fowl, and the waters yield their best fish: plentiful as these are with us, they are nothing in profusion to the kindly greeting and good wishes that fly about in the cold weather, and that circulate from land's end to land's end. The whole coast of England is surrounded by a general "shake hands." The coast-guard on their wintry walks do not greet each other more surely than old friends all over

151

England do: one clasps another, and another a third, till from Dover to London and so on to York, from Yarmouth on the east to Bristol on the west, from John O'Groat's house at the extreme north to the Land's End, the very toe-nail of England on the south—a kindly greeting, we may be sure, will pass. And a cheerful thing it is, on this day of universal equality, on this day which—

"To the cottage and the crown,
Brought tidings of salvation down,"

to think that we can touch and hold each other with friendly hands all over our land. We all of us shake hands on Christmas Day. Leigh Hunt had a quaint fancy that he had, as it were, by lineal descent, shaken hands with Milton. He would argue thus: he knew a man who had shaken hands with Dr. Johnson, who had clasped the hand of him who had shaken Dryden's right hand, who himself had thus greeted Andrew Marvell, who knew Master Elwood, the Quaker friend of Milton, who knew Milton himself; and thus, though our Sovereign has her hand kissed, not shaken, by her subjects, yet doubtless she will clasp the hands of her children, who, shaking those of others, will let the greeting and the good wishes descend to the lowest on that ladder of society which we are all trying to climb.

As for hearty good wishes, spoken in all kinds of voices, from the deepest bass to the shrillest treble, we are sure that they circulate throughout the little island, and are borne on the wings of the post all over the seas. Erasmus, coming to England in Henry VIII's time, was struck with the deep heartiness of our wishes—good, ay, and bad too; but he most admired the good ones. Other nations ask in their greetings how a man carries himself, or how doth he stand with the world, or how doth he find himself; but the English greet with a pious wish that God may give one a good morning or a good evening, good day, or "god'd'en," as the old writers have it; and when we part we wish that "God may be with you," though we now clip it into "Good b'ye."

A CHRISTMAS SONG

WILLIAM COX BENNETT

Blow, wind, blow,
Sing through yard and shroud;
Pipe it shrilly and loud,
Aloft as well as below;
Sing in my sailor's ear
The song I sing to you,
"Come home, my sailor true,
For Christmas that comes so near."

Go, wind, go,
Hurry his home-bound sail,
Through gusts that are edged with hail,
Through winter, and sleet, and snow;
Song, in my sailor's ear,
Your shrilling and moans shall be,
For he knows they sing him to me
And Christmas that comes so near.

SERY

RICHARD WATSON GILDER

With wild surprise
Four great eyes
In two small heads,
From neighboring beds
Looked out—and winked—
And glittered and blinked
At a very queer sight
In the dim starlight.

As plain as can be
A fairy tree
Flashes and glimmers
And shakes and shimmers.
Red, green and blue
Meet their view;
Silver and gold
Their sharp eyes behold;
Small moon, big stars;
And jams in jars,
And cakes, and honey
And thimbles, and money,
Pink dogs, blue cats,
Little squeaking rats,
And candles, and dolls,
And crackers, and polls,
A real bird that sings,
And tokens and favors,
And all sorts of things
For the little shavers.

Four black eyes
Grow big with surprise;
And then grow bigger
When a tiny figure,

154

Jaunty and airy,
(Is it a fairy?)
From the tree-top cries,
"Open wide! Black Eyes!
Come, children, wake now!
Your joys you may take now!"

Quick as you can think
Twenty small toes
In four pretty rows,
Like little piggies pink,
All kick in the air—
And before you can wink
The tree stands bare!

A CHRISTMAS SONG
TUDOR JENKS
When mother-love makes all things bright,
When joy comes with the morning light,
When children gather round their tree,
Thou Christmas Babe,
We sing of Thee!

When manhood's brows are bent in thought,
To learn what men of old have taught,
When eager hands seek wisdom's key,
Wise Temple Child,
We learn of Thee!

When doubts assail, and perils fright,
When, groping blindly in the night,
We strive to read life's mystery,
Man of the Mount,
We turn to Thee!

When shadows of the valley fall,

When sin and death the soul appall,
One light we through the darkness see—
Christ on the Cross,
We cry to Thee!

And when the world shall pass away,
And dawns at length the perfect day,
In glory shall our souls made free,
Thou God enthroned,
Then worship Thee.

CHRISTMAS
(A Selection from "Dreamthorp")
ALEXANDER SMITH

Sitting here, I incontinently find myself holding a levee of departed Christmas nights. Silently, and without special call, into my study of imagination come these apparitions, clad in snowy mantles, brooched and gemmed with frosts. Their numbers I do not care to count, for I know they are the numbers of many years. The visages of two or three are sad enough, but on the whole 'tis a congregation of jolly ghosts. The nostrils of my memory are assailed by a faint odor of plumpudding and burnt brandy. I hear a sound as of light music, a whisk of women's dresses whirled round in dance, a click as of glasses pledged by friends. Before one of these apparitions is a mound, as of a new-made grave, on which the snow is lying. I know, I know! Drape thyself not in white like the others, but in mourning stole of crape; and instead of dance music, let there haunt around thee the service for the dead! I know that sprig of mistletoe, O Spirit in the midst! Under it I swung the girl I loved—girl no more now than I am a boy—and kissed her spite of blush and pretty shriek. And thee, too, with fragrant trencher in hand, over which blue tongues of flame are playing, I do know—most ancient apparition of them all. I remember thy reigning night. Back to very days of childhood am I taken by the ghostly raisins simmering in a ghostly brandy flame. Where now the merry boys and girls that thrust their fingers in thy blaze? And now, when I think of it, thee also would I drape in black raiment, around thee also would I make the burial service murmur.

- - - - -

This, then, is Christmas, 1862. Everything is silent in Dreamthorp. The smith's hammer reposes beside the anvil. The weaver's flying shuttle is at rest. Through the clear wintry sunshine the bells this morning rang from the gray church tower amid the leafless elms, and up the walk the villagers trooped in their best dresses and their best faces—the latter a little

157

reddened by the sharp wind: mere redness in the middle aged; in the maids, wonderful bloom to the eyes of their lovers—and took their places decently in the ancient pews. The clerk read the beautiful prayers of our Church, which seem more beautiful at Christmas than at any other period. For that very feeling which breaks down at this time the barriers which custom, birth, or wealth have erected between man and man, strikes down the barrier of time which intervenes between the worshipper of to-day and the great body of worshippers who are at rest in their graves. On such a day as this, hearing these prayers, we feel a kinship with the devout generations who heard them long ago. The devout lips of the Christian dead murmured the responses which we now murmur; along this road of prayer did their thoughts of our innumerable dead, our brothers and sisters in faith and hope, approach the Maker, even as ours at present approach Him. Prayers over, the clergyman—who is no Boanerges, of Chrysostom, golden-mouthed, but a loving, genial-hearted, pious man, the whole extent of his life from boyhood until now, full of charity and kindly deeds, as autumn fields with heavy wheaten ears; the clergyman, I say—for the sentence is becoming unwieldy on my hands, and one must double back to secure connexion—read out in that silvery voice of his, which is sweeter than any music to my ear, those chapters of the New Testament that deal with the birth of the Saviour. And the red-faced rustic congregation hung on the good man's voice as he spoke of the Infant brought forth in a manger, of the shining angels that appeared in the mid-air to the shepherds, of the miraculous star that took its station in the sky, and of the wise men who came from afar and laid their gifts of frankincense and myrrh at the feet of the child. With the story every one was familiar, but on that day, and backed by the persuasive melody of the reader's voice, it seemed to all quite new—at least, they listened attentively as if it were. The discourse that followed possessed no remarkable thoughts; it dealt simply with the goodness of the Maker of heaven and earth, and the shortness of time, with the duties of

158

thankfulness and charity to the poor; and I am persuaded that every one who heard returned to his house in a better frame of mind. And so the service remitted us all to our own homes, to what roast-beef and plum-pudding slender means permitted, to gatherings around cheerful fires, to half-pleasant, half-sad remembrances of the dead and the absent.

From sermon I have returned like the others, and it is my purpose to hold Christmas alone. I have no one with me at table, and my own thoughts must be my Christmas guests. Sitting here, it is pleasant to think how much kindly feeling exists this present night in England. By imagination I can taste of every table, pledge every toast, silently join in every roar of merriment. I become a sort of universal guest. With what propriety is this jovial season, placed amid dismal December rains and snows! How one pities the unhappy Australians, with whom everything is turned topsy-turvy, and who holds Christmas at midsummer! The face of Christmas glows all the brighter for the cold. The heart warms as the frost increases. Estrangements which have embittered the whole year, melt in to-night's hospitable smile. There are warmer handshakings on this night than during the by-past twelve months. Friend lives in the mind of friend. There is more charity at this time than at any other. You get up at midnight and toss your spare coppers to the half-benumbed musicians whiffling beneath your windows, although at any other time you would consider their performance a nuisance, and call angrily for the police. Poverty, and scanty clothing, and fireless grates, come home at this season to the bosoms of the rich, and they give of their abundance. The very red-breast of the woods enjoys his Christmas feast. Good feeling incarnates itself into plum-pudding. The Master's words, "The poor ye have always with you," wear at this time a deep significance. For at least one night on each year over all Christendom there is brotherhood. And good men, sitting amongst their families, or by a solitary fire like me, when they remember the light, that shone over the poor clowns huddling on the Bethlehem plains eighteen hundred years ago, the apparition of shining angels overhead, the song "Peace on earth and good-will toward men," which for the first hallowed the midnight air,—pray for that strain's fulfilment, that battle and strife may vex the nations no more, that not only on Christmas eve, but the whole year round, men shall be brethren owning one Father in heaven.

- - - - -

Once again, for the purpose of taking away all solitariness of feeling, and of connecting myself, albeit only in fancy, with the proper gladness of the time, let me think of the comfortable family dinners now being drawn to a close, of the good wishes uttered, and the presents made, quite valueless in themselves, yet felt to be invaluable from the feelings from which they spring; of the little children, by sweetmeats lapped in Elysium; and of the pantomime, pleasantest Christmas sight of all, with the pit a sea of grinning delight, the boxes a tier of beaming juvenility, the galleries, piled up to the far-receding roof, a mass of happy laughter which a clown's joke brings down in mighty avalanches. In the pit, sober people relax themselves, and suck oranges, and quaff ginger-pop; in the boxes, Miss, gazing through her curls, thinks the Fairy Prince the prettiest creature she ever beheld, and Master, that to be a clown must be the pinnacle of human happiness: while up in the galleries the hard literal world is for an hour sponged out and obliterated; the chimney-sweep forgets, in his delight when the policeman comes to grief, the harsh call of his master, and Cinderella, when the demons are foiled, and the long parted lovers meet and embrace in a paradise of light and pink gauze, the grates that must be scrubbed to-morrow. All bands and trappings of toil are for one hour loosened by the hands of imaginative sympathy. What happiness a single theatre can contain! And those of maturer years, or of more meditative temperament, sitting at the pantomime, can extract out of the shifting scenes meanings suitable to themselves; for the pantomime is a symbol or adumbration of human life. Have we not all known Harlequin, who rules the roast, and has the pretty Columbine to

160

himself? Do we not all know that rogue of a clown with his peculating fingers, who brazens out of every scrape, and who conquers the world by good humour and ready wit? And have we not seen Pantaloons not a few, whose fate it is to get all the kicks and lose all the halfpence, to fall through all the trap doors, break their shins over all the barrows, and be forever captured by the policeman, while the true pilferer, the clown, makes his escape with the booty in his possession? Methinks I know the realities of which these things are but the shadows; have met with them in business, have sat with them at dinner. But to-night no such notions as these intrude; and when the torrent of fun, and transformation, and practical joking which rushed out of the beautiful fairy world gathered up again, the high-heaped happiness of the theatre will disperse itself, and the Christmas pantomime will be a pleasant memory the whole year through. Thousands on thousands of people are having their midriffs tickled at this moment; in fancy I see their lighted faces, in memory I see their mirth.

By this time I should think every Christmas dinner at Dreamthorp or elsewhere has come to an end. Even now in the great cities the theatres will be dispersing. The clown has wiped the paint off his face. Harlequin has laid aside his wand, and divested himself of his glittering raiment; Pantaloon, after refreshing himself with a pint of porter, is rubbing his aching joints; and Columbine, wrapped up in a shawl, and with sleepy eyelids, has gone home in a cab. Soon, in the great theatre, the lights will be put out, and the empty stage will be left to ghosts.

Hark! midnight from the church tower vibrates through the frosty air. I look out on the brilliant heaven, and see a milky way of powdery splendour wandering through it, and clusters and knots of stars and planets shining serenely in the blue frosty spaces; and the armed apparition of Orion, his spear pointing away into immeasurable space, gleaming overhead; and the familiar constellation of the Plough dipping down into the west; and I think when I go in again that there is one Christmas the less between me and my grave.

CHRISTMAS CAROL
PHILLIPS BROOKS

The earth has grown old with its burden of care,
But at Christmas it always is young,
The heart of the jewel burns lustrous and fair,
And its soul full of music bursts forth on the air,
When the song of the angels is sung.

It is coming, Old Earth, it is coming to-night!
On the snowflakes which cover thy sod
The feet of the Christ-child fall gentle and white,
And the voice of the Christ-child tells out with delight
That mankind are the children of God.

On the sad and the lonely, the wretched and poor,
The voice of the Christ-child shall fall;
And to every blind wanderer open the door
Of hope that he dared not to dream of before,
With a sunshine of welcome for all.

The feet of the humblest may walk in the field
Where the feet of the Holiest trod,
This, then, is the marvel to mortals revealed
When the silvery trumpets of Christmas have pealed,
That mankind are the children of God.

THE END OF THE PLAY
WILLIAM MAKEPEACE THACKERAY

The play is done—the curtain drops,
Slow-falling to the prompter's bell:
A moment yet the actor stops,
And looks around, to say farewell.
It is an irksome word and task;
And, when he's laughed and said his say,
He shows, as he removes his mask,

A face that's anything but gay.

One word, ere yet the evening ends,
   Let's close it with a parting rhyme;
And pledge a hand to all young friends,
   As fits the merry Christmas time.
On life's wide scene you, too, have parts
   That fate erelong shall bid you play;
Good-night!—with honest, gentle hearts
   A kindly greeting go alway!

Good-night!—I'd say the griefs, the joys,
   Just hinted in this mimic page,
The triumphs and defeats of boys,
   Are but repeated in our age.
I'd say your woes were not less keen,
Your hopes more vain than those of men,
   Your pangs or pleasures of fifteen
   At forty-five played o'er again.

I'd say we suffer and we strive,
   Not less nor more as men than boys,
With grizzled beards at forty-five
   As erst at twelve in corduroys;
And if, in time of sacred youth,
We learned at home to love and pray,
Pray Heaven that early love and truth
   May never wholly pass away.

And in the world as in the school
   I'd say how fate may change and shift,
The prize be sometimes to the fool,
   The race not always to the swift:
The strong may yield, the good may fall,
   The great man be a vulgar clown,
   The knave be lifted over all,

The kind cast pitilessly down.

Who knows the inscrutable design?
Blessèd be He who took and gave!
Why should your mother, Charles, not mine,
Be weeping at her darling's grave?
We bow to Heaven that willed it so,
That darkly rules the fate of all,
That sends the respite or the blow,
That's free to give or to recall.

This crowns his feast with wine and wit,—
Who brought him to that mirth and state?
His betters, see, below him sit,
Or hunger hopeless at the gate!
Who bade the mud from Dives's wheel
To spurn the rags of Lazarus?
Come, brother, in that dust we'll kneel,
Confessing Heaven that ruled it thus.

So each shall mourn, in life's advance,
Dear hopes, dear friends, untimely killed;
Shall grieve for many a forfeit chance,
And longing passion unfulfilled.
Amen!—whatever fate be sent,
Pray God the heart may kindly glow,
Although the head with cares be bent,
And whitened with the winter snow!

Come wealth or want, come good or ill,
Let young and old accept their part,
And bow before the awful will,
And bear it with an honest heart.
Who misses or who wins the prize,
Go, lose or conquer, as you can;
But if you fail, or if you rise,

Be each, pray God, a gentleman!

A gentleman, or old or young!
(Bear kindly with my humble lays;)
The sacred chorus first was sung
Upon the first of Christmas days;
The shepherds heard it overhead,—
The joyful angels raised it then:
"Glory to Heaven on high," it said,
"And peace on earth to gentle men!"

My song, save this, is little worth;
I lay the weary pen aside,
And wish you health and love and mirth,
As fits the solemn Christmas-tide.
As fits the holy Christmas birth,
Be this, good friends, our carol still:
Be peace on earth, be peace on earth
To men of gentle will!

CHRIST'S NATIVITY
HENRY VAUGHAN
Awake, glad heart! get up and sing!
It is the Birthday of thy King.
Awake! awake!
The sun doth shake
Light from his locks, and, all the way
Breathing perfumes, doth spice the day.

Awake! awake! hark how th' wood rings,
Winds whisper, and the busy springs
A concert make!
Awake! awake!
Man is their high-priest, and should rise
To offer up the sacrifice.

I would I were some bird, or star,
Fluttering in woods, or lifted far
Above this inn,
And road of sin!
Then either star or bird should be
Shining or singing still to thee.

I would I had in my best part
Fit rooms for thee! or that my heart
Where so clean as
Thy manger was!
But I am all filth, and obscene;
Yet, if thou wilt, thou canst make clean.

Sweet Jesu! will then. Let no more
This leper haunt and soil thy door!
Cure him, ease him,
O release him!
And let once more, by mystic birth,
The Lord of life be born in earth.

CHRISTMAS DREAMS
CHRISTOPHER NORTH

To-morrow is Merry Christmas; and when its night descends there will be mirth and music, and the light sounds of the merry-twinkling feet within these now so melancholy walls— and sleep now reigning over all the house save this one room, will be banished far over the sea—and morning will be reluctant to allow her light to break up the innocent orgies.

Were every Christmas of which we have been present at the celebration, painted according to nature—what a Gallery of Pictures! True that a sameness would pervade them all—but only that kind of sameness that pervades the nocturnal heavens. One clear night always is, to common eyes, just like another; for what hath any night to show but one moon and some stars—a blue vault, with here a few braided, and there a few castellated, clouds? yet no two nights ever bore more than a family resemblance to each other before the studious and instructed eye of him who has long communed with Nature, and is familiar with every smile and frown on her changeful, but not capricious, countenance. Even so with the Annual Festivals of the heart. Then our thoughts are the stars that illumine those skies—and on ourselves it depends whether they shall be black as Erebus, or brighter than Aurora.

"Thoughts! that like spirits trackless come and go"—is a fine line of Charles Lloyd's. But no bird skims, no arrow pierces the air, without producing some change in the Universe, which will last to the day of doom. No coming and going is absolutely trackless; nor irrecoverable by Nature's law is any consciousness, however ghostlike; though many a one, even the most blissful, never does return, but seems to be buried among the dead. But they are not dead—but only sleep; though to us who recall them not, they are as they had never been, and we, wretched ingrates, let them lie for ever in oblivion! How passing sweet when of their own accord they arise to greet us in our solitude!—as a friend who, having sailed away to a foreign land in our youth, has been thought to have died many long years ago, may suddenly stand before us, with face still familiar and name reviving in a moment, and all that he once was to us brought from utter forgetfulness close upon our heart.

My Father's House! How it is ringing like a grove in spring, with the din of creatures happier, a thousand times happier, than all the birds on earth. It is the Christmas Holidays—Christmas Day itself—Christmas Night—and Joy in every bosom intensifies Love. Never before were we brothers and sisters so dear to one another—never before had our hearts so yearned towards the authors of our being—our blissful being! There they sat—silent in all that outcry—composed in all that disarray—still in all that tumult; yet, as one or other flying imp sweeps round the chair, a father's hand will playfully strive to catch a prisoner—a mother's gentler touch on some sylph's disordered symar be felt almost as a reproof, and for a moment slacken the fairy flight. One old game treads on the heels of another—twenty within the hour—and many a new game never heard of before nor since, struck out by the collision of kindred spirits in their glee, the transitory fancies of genius inventive through very delight. Then, all at once, there is a hush, profound as ever falls on some little plat within a forest when the moon drops behind the mountain, and small green-robed People of Peace at once cease their pastime, and vanish. For she—the Silver-Tongued— is about to sing an old ballad, words and air alike hundreds of years old—and sing she doth, while tears begin to fall, with a voice too mournfully beautiful long to breathe below—and, ere another Christmas shall have come with the falling snows, doomed to be mute on earth—but to be hymning in Heaven.

Of that House—to our eyes the fairest of earthly dwellings— with its old ivyed turrets, and orchard-garden bright alike with fruit and with flowers, not one stone remains. The very brook that washed its foundations has vanished along with them—and a crowd of other buildings, wholly without character, has long stood where here a single tree, and there a grove, did once render so lovely that small demesne; which, how could we, who

168

thought it the very heart of Paradise, even for one moment have believed was one day to be blotted out of being, and we ourselves—then so linked in love that the band which bound us altogether was, in its gentle pressure, felt not nor understood—to be scattered far and abroad, like so many leaves that after one wild parting rustle are separated by roaring wind-eddies, and brought together no more! The old Abbey—it still survives; and there, in that corner of the burial-ground, below that part of the wall which was last in ruins, and which we often climbed to reach the flowers and nests—there, in hopes of a joyful resurrection, lie the Loved and Venerated—for whom, even now that so many grief-deadening years have fled, we feel, in this holy hour, as if it were impiety so utterly to have ceased to weep—so seldom to have remembered!—And then, with a powerlessness of sympathy to keep pace with youth's frantic grief, the floods we all wept together—at no long interval—on those pale and placid faces as they lay, most beautiful and most dreadful to behold, in their coffins.

We believe that there is genius in all childhood. But the creative joy that makes it great in its simplicity dies a natural death or is killed, and genius dies with it. In favored spirits, neither few nor many, the joy and the might survive; for you must know that unless it be accompanied with imagination, memory is cold and lifeless. The forms it brings before us must be inspired with beauty—that is, with affection or passion. All minds, even the dullest, remember the days of their youth; but all cannot bring back the indescribable brightness of that blessed season. They who would know what they once were, must not merely recollect but they must imagine, the hills and valleys—if any such there were—in which their childhood played, the torrents, the waterfalls, the lakes, the heather, the rocks, the heaven's imperial dome, the raven floating only a little lower than the eagle in the sky. To imagine what he then heard and saw, he must imagine his own nature. He must collect from many vanished hours the power of his untamed heart, and he must, perhaps, transfuse also something of his maturer mind into

these dreams of his former being, thus linking the past with the present by a continuous chain, which, though often invisible, is never broken. So is it too with the calmer affections that have grown within the shelter of a roof. We do not merely remember, we imagine our father's house, the fireside, all his features then most living, now dead and buried; the very manner of his smile, every tone of his voice. We must combine with all the passionate and plastic power of imagination the spirit of a thousand happy hours into one moment; and we must invest with all that we ever felt to be venerable such an image as alone can satisfy our filial hearts. It is thus that imagination, which first aided the growth of all our holiest and happiest affections, can preserve them to us unimpaired—
"For she can give us back the dead,
Even in the loveliest looks they wore."
Then came a New Series of Christmases, celebrated, one year in this family, another year in that—none present but those whom Charles Lamb the Delightful calleth the "old familiar faces;" something in all features, and all tones of voice, and all manners, betokening origin from one root—relations all, happy, and with no reason either to be ashamed or proud of their neither high nor humble birth, their lot being cast within that pleasant realm, "the Golden Mean," where the dwellings are connecting links between the hut and the hall—fair edifices resembling manse or mansion-house, according as the atmosphere expands or contracts their dimensions—in which Competence is next-door neighbor to Wealth, and both of them within the daily walk of Contentment.
Merry Christmases they were indeed—one Lady always presiding, with a figure that once had been the stateliest among the stately, but then somewhat bent, without being bowed down, beneath an easy weight of most venerable years. Sweet was her tremulous voice to all her grandchildren's ears. Nor did these solemn eyes, bedimmed into a pathetic beauty, in any degree restrain the glee that sparkled in orbs that had as yet shed not many tears, but tears of joy or pity. Dearly she loved

all those mortal creatures whom she was soon about to leave; but she sat in sunshine even within the shadow of death; and the "voice that called her home" had so long been whispering in her ear, that its accents had become dear to her, and consolatory every word that was heard in the silence, as from another world.

Whether we were indeed all so witty as we thought ourselves— uncles, aunts, brothers, sisters, nephews, nieces, cousins, and "the rest," it might be presumptuous in us, who were considered by ourselves and a few others not the least amusing of the whole set, at this distance of time to decide—especially in the affirmative; but how the roof did ring with sally, pun, retort, and repartee! Ay, with pun—a species of impertinence for which we have therefore a kindness even to this day. Had incomparable Thomas Hood had the good fortune to have been born a cousin of ours, how with that fine fancy of his would he have shone at those Christmas festivals, eclipsing us all! Our family, through all its different branches, has ever been famous for bad voices, but good ears; and we think we hear ourselves— all those uncles and aunts, nephews and nieces, and cousins— singing now! Easy it is to "warble melody" as to breathe air. But we hope harmony is the most difficult of all things to people in general, for to us it was impossible; and what attempts ours used to be at Seconds! Yet the most woful failures were rapturously encored; and ere the night was done we spoke with most extraordinary voices indeed, every one hoarser than another, till at last, walking home with a fair cousin, there was nothing left it but a tender glance of the eye—a tender pressure of the hand—for cousins are not altogether sisters, and although partaking of that dearest character, possess, it may be, some peculiar and appropriate charms of their own; as didst thou, Emily the "Wild-cap!"—That *soubriquet* all forgotten now—for now thou art a matron, nay a Grandam, and troubled with an elf fair and frolicsome as thou thyself wert of yore, when the gravest and wisest withstood not the witchery of thy dancings, thy singings, and thy showering smiles.

171

On rolled Suns and Seasons—the old died—the elderly became old—and the young, one after another, were wafted joyously away on the wings of hope, like birds almost as soon as they can fly, ungratefully forsaking their nests and the groves in whose safe shadow they first essayed their pinions; or like pinnaces that, after having for a few days trimmed their snow-white sails in the land-locked bay, close to whose shores of silvery sand had grown the trees that furnished timber both for hull and mast, slip their tiny cables on some summer day, and gathering every breeze that blows, go dancing over the waves in sunshine, and melt far off into the main. Or, haply, some were like fair young trees, transplanted during no favorable season, and never to take root in another soil, but soon leaf and branch to wither beneath the tropic sun, and die almost unheeded by those who knew not how beautiful they had been beneath the dews and mists of their own native climate.

Vain images! and therefore chosen by fancy not too plainly to touch the heart. For some hearts grew cold and forbidding with selfish cares—some, warm as ever in their own generous glow, were touched by the chill of Fortune's frowns, ever worst to bear when suddenly succeeding her smiles—some, to rid themselves of painful regrets, took refuge in forgetfulness, and closed their eyes to the past—duty banished some abroad, and duty imprisoned others at home—estrangements there were, at first unconscious and unintended, yet erelong, though causeless, complete—changes were wrought insensibly, invisibly, even in the innermost nature of those who being friends knew no guile, yet came thereby at last to be friends no more—unrequited love broke some bonds—requited love relaxed others—the death of one altered the conditions of many—and so—year after year—the Christmas Meeting was interrupted—deferred—till finally it ceased with one accord, unrenewed and unrenewable. For when Some Things cease for a time—that time turns out to be forever.

Survivors of those happy circles! wherever ye be—should these imperfect remembrances of days of old chance, in some

172

thoughtful pause of life's busy turmoil, for a moment to meet your eyes, let there be towards the inditer a few throbs of revived affection in your hearts—for his, though "absent long and distant far," has never been utterly forgetful of the loves and friendships that charmed his youth. To be parted in body is not to be estranged in spirit—and many a dream and many a vision, sacred to nature's best affections, may pass before the mind of one whose lips are silent. "Out of sight out of mind" is rather the expression of a doubt—of a fear—than a belief or a conviction. The soul surely has eyes that can see the objects it loves, through all intervening darkness—and of those more especially dear it keeps within itself almost undimmed images, on which, when they know it not, think it not, believe it not, it often loves to gaze, as on relics imperishable as they are hallowed.

All hail! rising beautiful and magnificent through the mists of morning—ye Woods, Groves, Towers, and Temples, overshadowing that famous Stream beloved by all the Muses! Through this midnight hush—methinks we hear faint and far-off sacred music—

"Where through the long-drawn aisle and fretted vault, The pealing anthem swells the note of praise!"

How steeped now in the stillness of moonlight are all those pale, pillared Churches, Courts and Cloisters, Shrines and Altars, with here and there a Statue standing in the shade, or Monument sacred to the memory of the pious—the immortal dead. Some great clock is striking from one of many domes—from the majestic Tower of St. Mary Magdalen—and in the deepened hush that follows the solemn sound, the mingling waters of the Cherwell and the Isis soften the severe silence of the holy night.

Remote from kindred, and from all the friendships that were the native growth of the fair fields where our boyhood and our youth had roamed and meditated and dreamed, those were indeed years of high and lofty mood which held us in converse with the shades of great Poets and ages of old in Rhedicyna's

173

hallowed groves, still, serene, and solemn, as that Attic Academe where divine Plato, with all Hybla on his lips, discoursed such excellent music that his life seemed to the imagination spiritualized—a dim reminiscence of some former state of being. How sank then the Christmas Service of that beautiful Liturgy into our hearts! Not faithless we to the simple worship that our forefathers had loved; but Conscience told us there was no apostasy in the feelings that rose within us when that deep organ began to blow, that choir of youthful voices so sweetly to join the diapason,—our eyes fixed all the while on that divine Picture over the Altar, of our Saviour

"Bearing his cross up rueful Calvary."

The City of Palaces disappears—and in the setting sunlight we behold mountains of soft crimson snow! The sun hath set, and even more beautiful are the bright-starred nights of winter, than summer in all its glories beneath the broad moons of June. Through the woods of Windermere, from cottage to cottage, by coppice-pathways winding up to dwellings among the hill-rocks where the birch-trees cease to grow—

"Nodding their heads, before us go,
The merry minstrelsy."

They sing a salutation at every door, familiarly naming old and young by their Christian names; and the eyes that look upward from the vales to the hanging huts among the plats and cliffs, see the shadows of the dancers ever and anon crossing the light of the star-like window, and the merry music is heard like an echo dwelling in the sky. Across those humble thresholds often did we on Christmas-week nights of yore—wandering through our solitary silvan haunts, under the branches of trees within whose hollow trunks the squirrel slept—venture in, unasked perhaps, but not unwelcome, and, in the kindly spirit of the season, did our best to merrify the Festival by tale or song. And now that we behold them not, are all those woods, and cliffs, and rivers, and tarns, and lakes, as beautiful as when they softened and brightened beneath our living eyes, half-creating, as they gazed, the very world they worshipped! And are all those hearths as bright as of yore, without the shadow of our figure! And the roofs, do they ring as mirthfully, though our voice be forgotten. We hang over Westmoreland, an unobserved—but observant star. Mountains, hills, rocks, knolls, vales, woods, groves, single trees, dwelling—all asleep! O Lakes! but we are indeed, by far too beautiful! O fortunate Isles! too fair for human habitation, fit abode for the Blest! It will not hide itself—it will not sink into the earth—it will rise; and risen, it will stand steady with its shadow in the overpowering moonlight, that ONE TREE! that ONE HOUSE!—and well might the sight of ye two together—were it harder—break our heart. But hard at all it is not—therefore it is but crushed.

Can it be that there we are utterly forgotten! No star hanging higher than the Andes in heaven—but sole-sitting at midnight in a small chamber—a melancholy man are we—and there seems a smile of consolation, O Wordsworth! on thy sacred Bust. Alas! how many heavenly days, "seeming immortal in their depth of rest," have died and been forgotten! Treacherous and ungrateful is our memory even of bliss that overflowed our being as light our habitation. Our spirit's deepest intercommunion with nature has no place in her records—blanks are there that ought to have been painted with imperishable imagery, and steeped in sentiment fresh as the morning on life's golden hills. Yet there is mercy in this dispensation—for who can bear to behold the light of bliss re-arising from the past on the ghastlier gloom of present misery? The phantoms that will not come when we call on them to comfort us, are too often at our side when in our anguish we could almost pray that they might be reburied in oblivion. Such hauntings as these are not as if they were visionary—they come and go like forms and shapes still imbued with life. Shall we vainly stretch out our arms to embrace and hold them fast, or as vainly seek to intrench ourselves by thought of this world against their visitation? The soul in its sickness knows not whether it be the duty of love to resign itself to indifference or to despair. Shall it enjoy life, they being dead? Shall we, the survivors, for yet a little while, walk in other companionship out into the day, and let the sunbeams settle on their heads as they used to do, or cover them with dust and ashes, and show to those in heaven that love for them is now best expressed by remorse and penitence?

Sometimes we have fears about our memory—that it is decaying; for, lately, many ordinary yet interesting occurrences and events, which we regarded at the time with pain or pleasure, have been slipping away almost into oblivion, and have often alarmed us of a sudden by their return, not to any act of recollection, but of themselves, sometimes wretchedly out of place and season, the mournful obtruding upon the merry, and worse, the merry upon the mournful—confusion, by no fault of ours, of piteous and gladsome faces—tears where smiles were a duty as well as a delight, and smiles where nature demanded, and religion hallowed, a sacrifice of tears.

For a good many years we have been tied to town in winter by fetters as fine as frost-work filigree, which we could not break without destroying a whole world of endearment. That seems an obscure image; but it means what the Germans would call in English—our winter environment. We are imprisoned in a net; yet we can see it when we choose—just as a bird can see, when he chooses, the wires of his cage, that are invisible in his happiness, as he keeps hopping and fluttering about all day long, or haply dreaming on his perch with his poll under his plumes—as free in confinement as if let loose into the boundless sky. That seems an obscure image too; but we mean, in truth, the prison unto which we doom ourselves no prison is; and we have improved on that idea, for we have built our own—and are prisoner, turnkey, and jailer all in one, and 'tis noiseless as the house of sleep. Or what if we declare that Christopher North is a king in his palace, with no subjects but his own thoughts—his rule peaceful over those lights and shadows—and undisputed to reign over them his right divine. The opening year in a town, now answers in all things to our heart's desire. How beautiful the smoky air! The clouds have a homely look as they hang over the happy families of houses, and seem as if they loved their birthplace;—all unlike those heartless clouds that keep *stravaiging* over mountain-tops, and have no domicile in the sky! Poets speak of living rocks, but what is their life to that of houses? Who ever saw a rock with eyes—that is, with windows? Stone-blind all, and stone-deaf, and with hearts of stone; whereas who ever saw a house without eyes—that is, windows? Our own is an Argus; yet the good old Conservative grudges not the assessed taxes—his optics are as cheerful as the day that lends them light, and they love to salute the setting sun, as if a hundred beacons, level above level, were kindled along a mountain side. He might safely be pronounced a madman who preferred an avenue of trees to a street. Why, trees have no chimneys; and, were you to kindle a fire in the hollow of an oak, you would soon be as dead as a Druid. It won't do to talk to us of sap, and the circulation of sap. A grove in winter, hole and branch—leaves it has none—is as dry as a volume of sermons. But a street, or a square, is full of "vital sparks of heavenly flame" as a volume of poetry, and the heart's blood circulates through the system like rosy wine.

But a truce to comparisons; for we are beginning to feel contrition for our crime against the country, and, with humbled head and heart, we beseech you to pardon us—ye rocks of Pavey-Ark, the pillared palaces of the storms—ye clouds, now wreathing a diadem for the forehead of Helvellyn—ye trees, that hang the shadows of your undying beauty over the "one perfect chrysolite," of blessed Windermere!

Our meaning is transparent now as the hand of an apparition waving peace and good-will to all dwellers in the land of dreams. In plainer but not simpler words (for words are like flowers, often rich in their simplicity—witness the Lily, and Solomon's Song)—Christian people all, we wish you a Merry Christmas and Happy New-Year, in town or in country—or in ships at sea.

KEEPING CHRISTMAS

Romans, xiv, 6: *He that regardeth the day, regardeth it unto the Lord,*

HENRY VAN DYKE

[From "The Spirit of Christmas."]

It is a good thing to observe Christmas day. The mere marking of times and seasons, when men agree to stop work and make merry together, is a wise and wholesome custom. It helps one to feel the supremacy of the common life over the individual life. It reminds a man to set his own little watch, now and then, by the great clock of humanity which runs on sun time.

But there is a better thing than the observance of Christmas day, and that is, keeping Christmas.

Are you willing to forget what you have done for other people, and to remember what other people have done for you; to ignore what the world owes you, and to think what you owe the world; to put your rights in the background, and your duties in the middle distance, and your chances to do a little more than your duty in the foreground; to see that your fellowmen are just as real as you are, and try to look behind their faces to their hearts, hungry for joy; to own that probably the only good reason for your existence is not what you are going to get out of life, but what you are going to give to life; to close your book of complaints against the management of the universe, and look around you for a place where you can sow a few seeds of happiness—are you willing to do these things even for a day?

Then you can keep Christmas.

Are you willing to stoop down and consider the needs and the desires of little children; to remember the weakness and loneliness of people who are growing old; to stop asking how much your friends love you, and ask yourself whether you love them enough; to bear in mind the things that other people have to bear in their hearts; to try to understand what those who live in the same house with you really want, without waiting for them to tell you; to trim your lamp so that it will give more light and less smoke, and to carry it in front so that your shadow will

178

fall behind you; to make a grave for your ugly thoughts and a garden for your kindly feelings, with the gate open—are you willing to do these things even for a day? Then you can keep Christmas.

Are you willing to believe that love is the strongest thing in the world—stronger than hate, stronger than evil, stronger than death—and that the blessed life which began in Bethlehem nineteen hundred years ago is the image and brightness of the Eternal Love? Then you can keep Christmas.

And if you keep it for a day, why not always?

But you can never keep it alone.

MARK WELL MY HEAVY DOLEFUL TALE
ANONYMOUS

Mark well my heavy doleful tale,
For Twelfth-day now is come,
And now I must no longer sing,
And say no words but mum;
For I perforce must take my leave
Of all my dainty cheer,
Plum-porridge, roast beef, and minced pies,
My strong ale and my beer.

Kind-hearted Christmas, now adieu,
For I with thee must part,
And for to take my leave of thee
Doth grieve me at the heart;
Thou wert an ancient housekeeper,
And mirth with meat didst keep,
But thou art going out of town,
Which makes me for to weep.

God knoweth whether I again
Thy merry face shall see,
Which to good-fellows and the poor
That was so frank and free.
Thou lovedst pastime with thy heart,
And eke good company;
Pray hold me up for fear I swoon,
For I am like to die.

Come, butler, fill a brimmer up
To cheer my fainting heart,
That to old Christmas I may drink
Before he doth depart;
And let each one that's in this room
With me likewise condole,
And for to cheer their spirits sad

Let each one drink a bowl.

And when the same it hath gone round
Then fall unto your cheer,
For you do know that Christmas time
It comes but once a year.
But this good draught which I have drunk
Hath comforted my heart,
For I was very fearful that
My stomach would depart.

Thanks to my master and my dame
That doth such cheer afford;
God bless them, that each Christmas they
May furnish thus their board.
My stomach having come to me,
I mean to have a bout,
Intending to eat most heartily;
Good friends, I do not flout.

A CHRISTMAS CAROL
CHRISTINA G. ROSSETTI
In the bleak mid-winter
Frosty wind made moan,
Earth stood hard as iron,
Water like a stone;
Snow had fallen, snow on snow,
Snow on snow,
In the bleak mid-winter
Long ago.

Our God, Heaven cannot hold him
Nor earth sustain;
Heaven and earth shall flee away,
When he comes to reign.
In the bleak mid-winter

A stable-place sufficed
The Lord God Almighty,
Jesus Christ.

Angels and archangels
May have gathered there;
Cherubim and seraphim
Thronged the air.
But only His Mother,
In her maiden bliss,
Worshipped her Beloved
With a kiss.

What can I give Him,
Poor as I am?
If I were a shepherd
I would bring a lamb;
If I were a wise man,
I would do my part,—
Yet what I can I give Him,
Give my heart.

THE GLORIOUS SONG OF OLD
EDMUND H. SEARS

It came upon the midnight clear,
That glorious song of old,
From angels bending near the earth
To touch their harps of gold,
"Peace on the earth, good-will to men,
From heaven's all-gracious King"—
The world in solemn stillness lay
To hear the angels sing.

Still through the cloven skies they come
With peaceful wings unfurled,
And still their heavenly music floats
O'er all the weary world;
Above its sad and lowly plains
They bend on hovering wing,
And ever o'er its Babel-sounds
The blessed angels sing.

But with the woes of sin and strife
The world has suffered long;
Beneath the angel-strain have rolled
Two thousand years of wrong.
And man at war with man hears not
The love-song which they bring;
Oh, hush the noise, ye men of strife,
And hear the angels sing!

And ye beneath life's crushing load,
Whose forms are bending low,
Who toil along the climbing way
With painful steps and slow,
Look now! for glad and golden hours
Come swiftly on the wing:—
Oh, rest beside the weary road

And hear the angels sing!

For lo! the days the hastening on
By prophet-bards foretold,
When with the ever-circling years
Comes round the age of gold;
When peace shall over all the earth
Its ancient splendors fling,
And the whole world give back the song
Which now the angels sing.

A CHRISTMAS CAROL FOR CHILDREN
MARTIN LUTHER

Good news from heaven the angels bring,
Glad tidings to the earth they sing:
To us this day a child is given,
To crown us with the joy of heaven.

This is the Christ, our God and Lord,
Who in all need shall aid afford:
He will Himself our Saviour be,
From sin and sorrow set us free.

To us that blessedness He brings,
Which from the Father's bounty springs:
That in the heavenly realm we may
With Him enjoy eternal day.

All hail, Thou noble Guest, this morn,
Whose love did not the sinner scorn!
In my distress Thou cam'st to me:
What thanks shall I return to Thee?

Were earth a thousand times as fair,
Beset with gold and jewels rare,
She yet were far too poor to be
A narrow cradle, Lord, for Thee.

Ah, dearest Jesus, Holy Child!
Make Thee a bed, soft, undefiled,
Within my heart, that it may be
A quiet chamber kept for Thee.

Praise God upon His heavenly throne,
Who gave to us His only Son:
For this His hosts, on joyful wing,
A blest New Year of mercy sing.

ON SANTA CLAUS
GEORGE A. BAKER, JR.

Brave old times those were. In the first half of the seventeenth century, we mean; before there was any such place as New York and Manhattan Island was occupied mostly by woods, and had a funny little Dutch town, known as New Amsterdam, sprouting out of the southern end of it. Those were the days of solid comfort, of mighty pipes, and unctuous doughnuts. Winter had not yet been so much affected by artificiality as he is now-a-days, and was contented to be what he is, not trying to pass himself off for Spring; and Christmas—well, it was Christmas. Do you know why? Because in those times Santa Claus used to live in a great old house in the midst of an evergreen forest, just back of the Hudson, and about half-way between New Amsterdam and Albany. A house built out of funny little Dutch bricks, with gables whose sides looked like stair-cases, and a roof of red tiles with more weathercocks and chimneys sticking out of it than you could count. Phew, how cold it was there! The wind roared and shouted around the house, and the snow fell steadily half the year, so that the summers never melted it away till winter came again. And Santa Claus thought that was the greatest pleasure in life: for he loved to have enormous fires in the great fire-places, and the colder it was, the bigger fires he would have, and the louder the winds roared around his chimney. There he sat and worked away all the year round, making dolls, and soldiers, and Noah's arks, and witches, and every other sort of toy you can think of. When Christmas Eve came he'd harness up his reindeers, Dasher, and Prancer, and Vixen, and the rest of them, and wrap himself up in furs, and light his big pipe, and cram his sled full of the doll-babies and Noah's arks, and all the other toys he'd been making, and off he'd go with a great shout and tremendous ringing of sleigh-bells. Before morning he'd be up and down every chimney in New Amsterdam, filling the stout grey yarn stockings with toys, and apples, and ginger-bread, laughing and chuckling so all the

186

while, that the laughs and chuckles didn't get out of the air for a week afterwards.

But the old house has gone to ruin, and Santa Claus doesn't live there any longer. You see he married about forty years ago; his wife was a Grundy, daughter of old Mrs. Grundy, of Fifth Avenue, of whom you've all heard. She married him for his money, and couldn't put up with his plain way of living and his careless jollity. He is such an easy-going, good natured old soul, that she manages him without any trouble. So the first thing she did was to make him change his name to St. Nicholas; then she made him give up his old house, and move into town; then she sent away the reindeers, for she didn't know what Ma *would* say to such an outlandish turn-out; then she threw away his pipe because it was vulgar, and the first Christmas Eve that he went off and stayed out all night she had hysterics, and declared she'd go home to her Ma, and get a divorce if he ever did such a thing again. She'd have put a stop to his giving away toys every year, too, only she thought it looked well, and as it was, she wouldn't let him make them himself any more, but compelled him to spend enormous sums in bringing them from Paris, and Vienna, and Nuremberg.

So now Santa Claus is St. Nicholas, and lives in a brown stone house on Fifth Avenue, a great deal handsomer than he can afford, and keeps a carriage, not because he wants it, but because Mrs. Shoddy, next door, keeps one; and loves, not to be jolly himself and to make everybody else so, but to please his wife's mother. He has to give an awful pull, what with his wife's extravagance, and the high prices of Parisian and Viennese toys, to make both ends meet, although he does speculate in stocks, and is very lucky. Instead of looking forward to Christmas with pleasure, and thinking what a good time he will have, he pulls out his ledger, and groans, and wonders how on earth he's going to make his presents this year, and thinks he would stop giving them entirely, only he's so mortally afraid of his mother-in-law, and he knows what she'd say if he did. So he borrows money wherever he can, and sends over to Paris for fans, and opera-glasses, and bon-bon boxes, and jewelry, and when they come he sits down in his parlor and lets his wife tell him just what to do with them. So she takes out her list and runs over the names; she has all the rich people down, for she is a religious woman, and the Bible says "unto him that hath, it shall be given." This is the way she talks: "The little Croesuses must have some very elegant things, of course; their mother's a horrid old cat, but Croesus could help you very much in business. And there are the Centlivres; we must pick out something magnificent for them; they give a party Christmas night: of course the presents will be on exhibition, and I shall sink with shame if any one else's are handsomer than ours." So she goes on, until all the rich people are disposed of. Then Santa Claus asks: "How about the Brinkers, my dear?" The Brinkers are great favorites of his. "Good gracious, dearest! How often have I told you, you mustn't manifest such an interest in those Brinkers? What would Ma say if she knew you associated with such common people!" "But, I'm Dutch myself, pet." "Of course you are, darling, but there's no need of letting every one know it!" St. Nicholas hardly dares to do it, but he finally suggests very meekly: "The poor children, my darling." "Bother the poor children, my dear!" They're a most affectionate couple, you know. Then St. Nicholas sighs and sighs, and sends for his messengers, and they all come in with long faces, and take off big packages to the Croesuses and the Centlivres, and the rest of them. The messengers do their work entirely as a matter of business, so there isn't a sign of a laugh, nor a symptom of a chuckle in the air next day. The little Croesuses first cry, because they haven't received more, and then fight over what they have; then they eat too much French candy, and get sick and cross, and the whole house is filled with their noise. So mamma has a headache; and papa longs for his office, and misses the tick-tick of the stock telegraph, and thinks what a confounded nuisance holidays are. That is what Christmas is like in good society.

188

But I must tell you a secret. Away up in the fourth-story of his grand house, where his wife never goes, St. Nicholas has a little workshop, and there he sits whenever he gets a chance, making the most wonderful dolls, and gorgeous soldiers, and miraculous jumping-jacks, and tin horns—such quantities of tin horns! Some one ought to speak to him about those tin horns. But after all they please the poor children, so we suppose it's all right. Now do you know what he does with these things? On Christmas Eve he gets his old sled down from the stable away up by the North Pole, and as soon as his wife is fast asleep, he puts on his old furs and gets out from under his shirts in his bureau drawer a Dutch pipe, three times as big as the one his wife threw away, and off he goes. He tumbles down all the poor people's chimneys, and fills up the stockings to overflowing, and plants gorgeous Christmas trees in all the Mission schools.

He has a glorious good time, and laughs and chuckles tremendously, except when, once in a while, he thinks of what would happen if his wife found him out.

So there's a little fun going on after all.

Do you know, if it were not for this performance of his, we should wish with all our heart that St. Nicholas were dead and buried. But we must say, we wish his wife would die, and that all the Grundy family would follow her good example, for between them they've spoiled a good many jolly people besides St. Nicholas.

A CHRISTMAS CAROL

JOSIAH GILBERT HOLLAND

There's a song in the air!
There's a star in the sky!
There's a mother's deep prayer
And a baby's low cry!
And the star rains its fire while the Beautiful sing,
For the manger of Bethlehem cradles a king.

There's a tumult of joy
O'er the wonderful birth,
For the virgin's sweet boy
Is the Lord of the earth,
Ay! the star rains its fire and the Beautiful sing,
For the manger of Bethlehem cradles a king.

In the light of that star
Lie the ages impearled;
And that song from afar
Has swept over the world.
Every hearth is aflame, and the Beautiful sing
In the homes of the nations that Jesus is King.

We rejoice in the light,
And we echo the song
That comes down through the night
From the heavenly throng.
Ay! we shout to the lovely evangel they bring,
And we greet in his cradle our Saviour and King!

AN OFFERTORY

MARY MAPES DODGE

Oh, the beauty of the Christ Child,
The gentleness, the grace,
The smiling, loving tenderness,
The infantile embrace!
All babyhood he holdeth,
All motherhood enfoldeth—
Yet who hath seen his face?

Oh, the nearness of the Christ Child,
When, for a sacred space,
He nestles in our very homes—
Light of the human race!
We know him and we love him,
No man to us need prove him—
Yet who hath seen his face?

CHRISTMAS SONG
LYDIA A.C. WARD

Why do bells for Christmas ring?
Why do little children sing?

Once a lovely, shining star,
Seen by shepherds from afar,
Gently moved until its light
Made a manger-cradle bright.

There a darling baby lay
Pillowed soft upon the hay.
And his mother sang and smiled,
"This is Christ, the holy child."

So the bells for Christmas ring,
So the little children sing.

A CHRISTMAS CAROL
CHRISTIAN BURKE

The trees are hung with crystal lamps, the world lies still and
white,
And the myriad little twinkling stars are sharp with keener light;
The moon sails up the frost-clear sky and silvers all the snow,
As she did, perchance, that Christmas night, two thousand years
ago!
Good people, are you waking?
Give us food and give us wine,
For the sake of blessed Mary
And her Infant Son Divine,
Who was born the world's Redeemer—
A Saviour—yours and mine!

Long ago angelic harpers sang the song we sing to-day,
And the drowsy folk of Bethlehem may have listened as they
lay!
But eager shepherds left their flocks, and o'er the desert wild
The kingly sages journeyed to adore the Holy Child!
Has any man a quarrel?
Has another used you ill?
The friendly word you meant to say,
Is that unspoken still?—
Then, remember, 'twas the Angels
Brought glad tidings of good will!

Of all the gifts of Christmas, are you fain to win the best?
Lo! the Christ-child still is waiting Himself to be your guest;
No lot so high or lowly but He will take His part,
If you do but bid Him welcome to a clean and tender heart.
Are you sleeping, are you waking?
To the Manger haste away,
And you shall see a wond'rous sight
Amid the straw and hay.—

193

'Tis Love Himself Incarnate
As on this Christmas Day!

A SIMPLE BILL OF FARE FOR A CHRISTMAS DINNER
H.H.

All good recipe-books give bills of fare for different occasions, bills of fare for grand dinners, bills of fare for little dinners; dinners to cost so much per head; dinners "which can be easily prepared with one servant," and so on. They give bills of fare for one week; bills of fare for each day in a month, to avoid too great monotony in diet. There are bills of fare for dyspeptics; bills of fare for consumptives; bills of fare for fat people, and bills of fare for thin; and bills of fare for hospitals, asylums, and prisons, as well as for gentlemen's houses. But among them all, we never saw the one which we give below. It has never been printed in any book; but it has been used in families. We are not drawing on our imagination for its items. We have sat at such dinners; we have helped prepare such dinners; we believe in such dinners; they are within everybody's means. In fact, the most marvellous thing about this bill of fare is that the dinner does not cost a cent. Ho! all ye that are hungry and thirsty, and would like so cheap a Christmas dinner, listen to this:

BILL OF FARE FOR A CHRISTMAS DINNER
First Course—Gladness.

This must be served hot. No two housekeepers make it alike; no fixed rule can be given for it. It depends, like so many of the best things, chiefly on memory; but, strangely enough, it depends quite as much on proper forgetting as on proper remembering. Worries must be forgotten. Troubles must be forgotten. Yes, even sorrow itself must be denied and shut out. Perhaps this is not quite possible. Ah! we all have seen Christmas days on which sorrow would not leave our hearts nor our houses. But even sorrow can be compelled to look away from its sorrowing for a festival hour which is so solemnly joyous at Christ's Birthday. Memory can be filled full of other things to be remembered. No soul is entirely destitute of blessings, absolutely without comfort. Perhaps we have but one. Very well; we can think steadily of that one, if we try. But the probability is that we have more than we can count. No man has yet numbered the blessings, the mercies, the joys of God. We are all richer than we think; and if we once set ourselves to reckoning up the things of which we are glad, we shall be astonished at their number.

Gladness, then, is the first item, the first course on our bill of fare for a Christmas dinner.

Entrées—Love garnished with Smiles.

GENTLENESS, with sweet-wine sauce of Laughter.

GRACIOUS SPEECH, cooked with any fine, savory herbs, such as Frollery, which is always in season, or Pleasant Reminiscence, which no one need be without, as it keeps for years, sealed or unsealed.

Second Course—HOSPITALITY.

The precise form of this also depends on individual preferences. We are not undertaking here to give exact recipes, only a bill of fare.

In some houses Hospitality is brought on surrounded with Relatives. This is very well. In others, it is dished up with Dignitaries of all sorts; men and women of position and estate for whom the host has special likings or uses. This gives a fine effect to the eye, but cools quickly, and is not in the long-run satisfying.

In a third class, best of all, it is served in simple shapes, but with a great variety of Unfortunate Persons,—such as lonely people from lodging-houses, poor people of all grades, widows and childless in their affliction. This is the kind most preferred; in fact, never abandoned by those who have tried it.

For Dessert—MIRTH, in glasses.

GRATITUDE and FAITH beaten together and piled up in snowy shapes. These will look light if run over night in the moulds of Solid Trust and Patience.

A dish of the bonbons Good Cheer and Kindliness with every-day mottoes; Knots and Reasons in shape of Puzzles and Answers; the whole ornamented with Apples of Gold in Pictures of Silver, of the kind mentioned in the Book of Proverbs.

This is a short and simple bill of fare. There is not a costly thing in it; not a thing which cannot be procured without difficulty. If meat be desired, it can be added. That is another excellence about our bill of fare. It has nothing in it which makes it incongruous with the richest or the plainest tables. It is not overcrowded by the addition of roast goose and plum-pudding; it is not harmed by the addition of herring and potatoes. Nay, it can give flavor and richness to broken bits of stale bread served on a doorstep and eaten by beggars.

We might say much more about this bill of fare. We might, perhaps, confess that it has an element of the supernatural; that its origin is lost in obscurity; that, although, as we said, it has never been printed before, it has been known in all ages; that the martyrs feasted upon it; that generations of the poor, called blessed by Christ, have laid out banquets by it; that exiles and prisoners have lived on it; and the despised and forsaken and rejected in all countries have tasted it. It is also true that when any great king ate well and throve on his dinner, it was by the same magic food. The young and the free and the glad, and all rich men in costly houses, even they have not been well fed without it.

And though we have called it a Bill of Fare for a Christmas Dinner, that is only that men's eyes may be caught by its name, and that they, thinking it a specialty for festival, may learn and understand its secret, and henceforth, laying all their dinners according to its magic order, may "eat unto the Lord."

A BALLADE OF OLD LOVES
CAROLYN WELLS

Who is it stands on the polished stair,
A merry, laughing, winsome maid,
From the Christmas rose in her golden hair
To the high-heeled slippers of spangled suède
A glance, half daring and half afraid,
Gleams from her roguish eyes downcast;
Already the vision begins to fade—
'Tis only a ghost of a Christmas Past.

Who is it sits in that high-backed chair,
Quaintly in ruff and patch arrayed,
With a mockery gay of a stately air
As she rustles the folds of her old brocade,—
Merriest heart at the masquerade?
Ah, but the picture is passing fast
Back to the darkness from which it strayed—
'Tis only a ghost of a Christmas Past.

Who is it whirls in a ball-room's glare,
Her soft white hand on my shoulder laid,
Like a radiant lily, tall and fair,
While the violins in the corner played
The wailing strains of the Serenade?
Oh, lovely vision, too sweet to last—
E'en now my fancy it will evade—
'Tis only a ghost of a Christmas Past.

L'ENVOI

Rosamond! look not so dismayed,
All of my heart, dear love, thou hast
Jealous, beloved? Of a shade?—
'Tis only a ghost of a Christmas Past.

BALLADE OF CHRISTMAS GHOSTS
ANDREW LANG

Between the moonlight and the fire
In winter twilights long ago,
What ghosts we raised for your desire,
To make your merry blood run slow!
How old, how grave, how wise we grow!
No Christmas ghost can make us chill,
Save those that troop in mournful row,
The ghosts we all can raise at will!

The beasts can talk in barn and byre
On Christmas Eve, old legends know.
As year by year the years retire,
We men fall silent then I trow,
Such sights hath memory to show,
Such voices from the silence thrill,
Such shapes return with Christmas snow,—
The ghosts we all can raise at will.

Oh, children of the village choir,
Your carols on the midnight throw,
Oh, bright across the mist and mire,
Ye ruddy hearths of Christmas glow!
Beat back the dread, beat down the woe,
Let's cheerily descend the hill;
Be welcome all, to come or go,
The ghosts we all can raise at will.

ENVOY

Friend, sursum corda, soon or slow
We part, like guests who've joyed their fill;
Forget them not, nor mourn them so,
The ghosts we all can raise at will.

HANG UP THE BABY'S STOCKING

[Emily Huntington Miller]

Hang up the baby's stocking:
Be sure you don't forget;
The dear little dimpled darling!
She ne'er saw Christmas yet;
But I've told her all about it,
And she opened her big blue eyes,
And I'm sure she understood it—
She looked so funny and wise.

Dear! what a tiny stocking!
It doesn't take much to hold
Such little pink toes as baby's
Away from the frost and cold.
But then for the baby's Christmas
It will never do at all;
Why, Santa wouldn't be looking
For anything half so small.

I know what will do for the baby.
I've thought of the very best plan:
I'll borrow a stocking of grandma,
The longest that ever I can;
And you'll hang it by mine, dear mother,
Right here in the corner, so!
And write a letter to Santa,
And fasten it on to the toe.

Write, "This is the baby's stocking
That hangs in the corner here;
You never have seen her, Santa,
For she only came this year;
But she's just the blessedest baby!
And now, before you go,

Just cram her stocking with goodies,
From the top clean down to the toe."

THE NEWEST THING IN CHRISTMAS CAROLS
ANONYMOUS

God rest you, merry gentlemen!
May nothing you dismay;
Not even the dyspeptic plats
Through which you'll eat your way;
Nor yet the heavy Christmas bills
The season bids you pay;
No, nor the ever tiresome need
Of being to order gay;

Nor yet the shocking cold you'll catch
If fog and slush hold sway;
Nor yet the tumbles you must bear
If frost should win the day;
Nor sleepless nights—they're sure to come—
When "waits" attune their lay;
Nor pantomimes, whose dreariness
Might turn macassar gray;

Nor boisterous children, home in heaps,
And ravenous of play;
Nor yet—in fact, the host of ills
Which Christmases array.
God rest you, merry gentlemen,
May none of these dismay!

A CHRISTMAS LETTER FROM AUSTRALIA
DOUGLAS SLADEN

'Tis Christmas, and the North wind blows; 'twas two years
yesterday
Since from the Lusitania's bows I looked o'er Table Bay,
A tripper round the narrow world, a pilgrim of the main,
Expecting when her sails unfurled to start for home again.

'Tis Christmas, and the North wind blows; to-day our hearts are
one,
Though you are 'mid the English snows and I in Austral sun;
You, when you hear the Northern blast, pile high a mightier fire,
Our ladies cower until it's past in lawn and lace attire.

I fancy I can picture you upon this Christmas night,
Just sitting as you used to do, the laughter at its height;
And then a sudden, silent pause intruding on your glee,
And kind eyes glistening because you chanced to think of me.

This morning when I woke and knew 'twas Christmas come
again,
I almost fancied I could view white rime upon the pane,
And hear the ringing of the wheels upon the frosty ground,
And see the drip that downward steals in icy casket bound.

I daresay you'll be on the lake, or sliding on the snow,
And breathing on your hands to make the circulation flow,
Nestling your nose among the furs of which your boa's made,—
The Fahrenheit here registers a hundred in the shade.

It is not quite a Christmas here with this unclouded sky,
This pure transparent atmosphere, this sun mid-heaven-high;
To see the rose upon the bush, young leaves upon the trees,
And hear the forest's summer hush or the low hum of bees.

But cold winds bring not Christmastide, nor budding roses June,

And when it's night upon your side we're basking in the noon.
Kind hearts make Christmas—June can bring blue sky or clouds
above;
The only universal spring is that which comes of love.

And so it's Christmas in the South as on the North-sea coasts,
Though we are staved with summer-drouth and you with winter
frosts.
And we shall have our roast beef here, and think of you the
while,
Though all the watery hemisphere cuts off the mother isle.

Feel sure that we shall think of you, we who have wandered
forth,
And many a million thoughts will go to-day from south to north;
Old heads will muse on churches old, where bells will ring to-
day—
The very bells, perchance, which tolled their fathers to the clay.

And now, good-night! and I shall dream that I am with you all,
Watching the ruddy embers gleam athwart the panelled hall;
Nor care I if I dream or not, though severed by the foam,
My heart is always in the spot which was my childhood's home.

CHRISTMAS
ROSE TERRY COOKE

Here comes old Father Christmas,
With sound of fife and drums;
With mistletoe about his brows,
So merrily he comes!
His arms are full of all good cheer,
His face with laughter glows,
He shines like any household fire
Amid the cruel snows.
He is the old folks' Christmas;
He warms their hearts like wine;
He thaws their winter into spring,
And makes their faces shine.
Hurrah for Father Christmas!
Ring all the merry bells!
And bring the grandsires all around
To hear the tale he tells.

Here comes the Christmas angel,
So gentle and so calm;
As softly as the falling flakes
He comes with flute and psalm.
All in a cloud of glory,
As once upon the plain
To shepherd-boys in Jewry,
He brings good news again.
He is the young folks' Christmas;
He makes their eyes grow bright
With words of hope and tender thought,
And visions of delight.
Hail to the Christmas angel!
All peace on earth he brings;
He gathers all the youths and maids
Beneath his shining wings.

Here comes the little Christ-child,
All innocence and joy,
And bearing gifts in either hand
For every girl and boy.
He tells the tender story
About the Holy Maid,
And Jesus in the manger
Before the oxen laid.
Like any little winter bird
He sings his sweetest song,
Till all the cherubs in the sky
To hear his carol throng.
He is the children's Christmas;
They come without a call,
To gather round the gracious Child,
Who bringeth joy to all.

But who shall bring *their* Christmas
Who wrestle still with life?
Not grandsires, youths, or little folks,
But they who wage the strife—
The fathers and the mothers
Who fight for homes and bread,
Who watch and ward the living,
And bury all the dead?
Ah! by their side at Christmas-tide
The Lord of Christmas stands:
He smooths the furrows from their brow
With strong and tender hands.
"I take my Christmas gift," He saith,
"From thee, tired soul, and he
Who giveth to My little ones
Gives also unto Me."

IV

STORIES

THE FIR TREE
HANS CHRISTIAN ANDERSEN

Out in the forest stood a pretty little Fir Tree. It had a good place; it could have sunlight, air there was in plenty, and all around grew many larger comrades—pines as well as firs. But the little Fir Tree wished ardently to become greater. It did not care for the warm sun and the fresh air; it took no notice of the peasant children, who went about talking together, when they had come out to look for strawberries and raspberries. Often they came with a whole pot-full, or had strung berries on a straw; then they would sit down by the little Fir Tree and say, "How pretty and small that one is!" and the Tree did not like to hear that at all.

Next year he had grown a great joint, and the following year he was longer still, for in fir trees one can always tell by the number of rings they have how many years they have been growing.

"Oh, if I were only as great a tree as the others!" sighed the little Fir, "then I would spread my branches far around, and look out from my crown into the wide world. The birds would then build nests in my boughs, and when the wind blew I could nod just as grandly as the others yonder."

He took no pleasure in the sunshine, in the birds, and in the red clouds that went sailing over him morning and evening.

When it was winter, and the snow lay all around, white and sparkling, a hare would often come jumping along, and spring right over the little Fir Tree. Oh! this made him so angry. But two winters went by, and when the third came the little Tree had grown so tall that the hare was obliged to run around it. "Oh! to grow, to grow, and become old; that's the only fine thing in the world," thought the Tree.

In the autumn woodcutters always came and felled a few of the largest trees; that was done this year too, and the little Fir Tree, that was now quite well grown, shuddered with fear, for the great stately trees fell to the ground with a crash, and their branches were cut off, so that the trees looked quite naked, long, and slender—they could hardly be recognized. But then they were laid upon waggons, and horses dragged them away out of the wood. Where were they going? What destiny awaited them?

In the spring, when the swallows and the Stork came, the Tree asked them, "Do you know where they were taken? Did you not meet them?"

The swallows knew nothing about it, but the Stork looked thoughtful, nodded his head, and said,

"Yes, I think so. I met many new ships when I flew out of Egypt; on the ships were stately masts; I fancy that these were the trees. They smelt like fir. I can assure you they're stately—very stately."

"Oh that I were only big enough to go over the sea! What kind of thing is this sea, and how does it look?"

"It would take too long to explain all that," said the Stork, and he went away.

"Rejoice in thy youth," said the Sunbeams; "rejoice in thy fresh growth, and in the young life that is within thee."

And the wind kissed the Tree, and the dew wept tears upon it; but the Fir Tree did not understand that.

When Christmas-time approached, quite young trees were felled, sometimes trees which were neither so old nor so large as this Fir Tree, that never rested but always wanted to go away. These young trees, which were almost the most beautiful, kept all their branches; they were put upon wagons, and horses dragged them away out of the wood.

"Where are they all going?" asked the Fir Tree. "They are not greater than I—indeed, one of them was much smaller. Why do they keep all their branches? Whither are they taken?"

"We know that! We know that!" chirped the Sparrows. "Yonder in the town we looked in at the windows. We know where they go. Oh! they are dressed up in the greatest pomp and splendor that can be imagined. We have looked in at the windows, and have perceived that they are planted in the middle of the warm room, and adorned with the most beautiful things—gilt apples, honey-cakes, playthings, and many hundreds of candles."

"And then?" asked the Fir Tree, and trembled through all its branches. "And then? What happens then?"

"Why, we have not seen anything more. But it was incomparable."

"Perhaps I may be destined to tread this glorious path one day!" cried the Fir Tree rejoicingly. "That is even better than traveling across the sea. How painfully I long for it! If it were only Christmas now! Now I am great and grown up, like the rest who were led away last year. Oh, if I were only on the carriage! If I were only in the warm room, among all the pomp and splendor! And then? Yes, then something even better will come, something far more charming, or else why should they adorn me so? There must be something grander, something greater still to come; but what? Oh, I'm suffering, I'm longing! I don't know myself what is the matter with me!"

"Rejoice in us," said Air and Sunshine, "Rejoice in thy fresh youth here in the woodland."

But the Fir Tree did not rejoice at all, but it grew and grew; winter and summer it stood there, green, dark green. The people who saw it said, "That's a handsome tree!" and at Christmas-time it was felled before any one of the others. The axe cut deep into its marrow, and the tree fell to the ground with a sigh: it felt a pain, a sensation of faintness, and could not think at all of happiness, for it was sad at parting from its home, from the place where it had grown up: it knew that it should never again see the dear old companions, the little bushes and flowers all around—perhaps not even the birds. The parting was not at all agreeable.

The Tree only came to itself when it was unloaded in a yard, with other trees, and heard a man say,

"This one is famous; we only want this one!"

Now two servants came in gay liveries, and carried the Fir Tree into a large beautiful saloon. All around the walls hung pictures, and by the great stove stood large Chinese vases with lions on the covers; there were rocking-chairs, silken sofas, great tables covered with picture-books, and toys worth a hundred times a hundred dollars, at least the children said so. And the Fir Tree was put into a great tub filled with sand; but no one could see that it was a tub, for it was hung round with green cloth, and stood on a large many-colored carpet. Oh, how the Tree trembled! What was to happen now? The servants, and the young ladies also, decked it out. On one branch they hung little nets, cut out of colored paper; every net was filled with sweetmeats; golden apples and walnuts hung down as if they grew there, and more than a hundred little candles, red, white, and blue, were fastened to the different boughs. Dolls that looked exactly like real people—the Tree had never seen such before—swung among the foliage, and high on the summit of the Tree was fixed a tinsel star. It was splendid, particularly splendid.

"This evening," said all, "this evening it will shine."

"Oh," thought the Tree, "that it were evening already! Oh that the lights may be soon lit up! When may that be done? I wonder if trees will come out of the forest to look at me? Will the sparrows fly against the panes? Shall I grow fast here, and stand adorned in summer and winter?"

Yes, he did not guess badly. But he had a complete backache from mere longing, and the backache is just as bad for a Tree as the headache for a person.

At last the candles were lighted. What a brilliance, what splendor! The Tree trembled so in all its branches that one of the candles set fire to a green twig, and it was scorched.

"Heaven preserve us!" cried the young ladies; and they hastily put the fire out.

Now the Tree might not even tremble. Oh, that was terrible! It was so afraid of setting fire to some of its ornaments, and it was quite bewildered with all the brilliance. And now the folding doors were thrown open, and a number of children rushed in as if they would have overturned the whole Tree; the older people followed more deliberately. The little ones stood quite silent, but only for a minute; then they shouted till the room rang: they danced gleefully round the Tree, and one present after another was plucked from it.

"What are they about?" laughed the Tree. "What's going to be done?"

And the candles burned down to the twigs, and as they burned down they were extinguished, and then the children received permission to plunder the Tree. Oh! they rushed in upon it, so that every branch cracked again: if it had not been fastened by the top and by the golden star to the ceiling, it would have fallen down.

The children danced about with their pretty toys. No one looked at the Tree except one old man, who came up and peeped among the branches, but only to see if a fig or an apple had not been forgotten.

"A story! a story!" shouted the children: and they drew a little fat man towards the Tree; and he sat down just beneath it,— "for then we shall be in the green wood," said he, "and the tree may have the advantage of listening to my tale. But I can only tell one. Will you hear the story of Ivede-Avede, or of Klumpey-Dumpey, who fell down stairs, and still was raised up to honor and married the Princess?"

"Ivede-Avede!" cried some, "Klumpey-Dumpey!" cried others, and there was a great crying and shouting. Only the Fir Tree was quite silent, and thought, "Shall I not be in it? shall I have nothing to do in it?" But he had been in the evening's amusement, and had done what was required of him.

And the fat man told about Klumpey-Dumpey, who fell down stairs, and yet was raised to honor and married the Princess. And the children clapped their hands, and cried, "Tell another! tell another!" for they wanted to hear about Ivede-Avede; but they only got the story of Klumpey-Dumpey. The Fir Tree stood quite silent and thoughtful; never had the birds in the wood told such a story as that. Klumpey-Dumpey fell down stairs, and yet came to honor and married the Princess!

"Yes, so it happens in the world!" thought the Fir Tree, and believed it must be true, because that was such a nice man who told it. "Well, who can know? Perhaps I shall fall down stairs too, and marry a Princess!" And it looked forward with pleasure to being adorned again, the next evening, with candles and toys, gold and fruit. "To-morrow I shall not tremble," it thought. "I will rejoice in all my splendor. To-morrow I shall hear the story of Klumpey-Dumpey again, and, perhaps, that of Ivede-Avede too."

And the Tree stood all night quiet and thoughtful.

In the morning the servants and the chambermaid came in. "Now my splendor will begin afresh," thought the Tree. But they dragged him out of the room, and up stairs to the garret, and here they put him in a dark corner where no daylight shone. "What's the meaning of this?" thought the Tree. "What am I to do here? What is to happen?"

And he leaned against the wall, and thought, and thought. And he had time enough, for days and nights went by, and nobody came up; and when at length some one came, it was only to put some great boxes in a corner. Now the Tree stood quite hidden away, and the supposition was that it was quite forgotten.

"Now it's winter outside," thought the Tree. "The earth is hard and covered with snow, and people cannot plant me; therefore I suppose I'm to be sheltered here until spring comes. How considerate that is! How good people are! If it were only not so dark here, and so terribly solitary!—not even a little hare! That was pretty out there in the wood, when the snow lay thick and the hare sprang past; yes, even when he jumped over me; but then I did not like it. It is terribly lonely up here!"

"Piep! piep!" said a little Mouse, and crept forward, and then came another little one. They smelt at the Fir Tree, and then slipped among the branches.

"It's horribly cold," said the two little Mice, "or else it would be comfortable here. Don't you think so, you old Fir Tree?"

211

"I'm not old at all," said the Fir Tree. "There are many much older than I."

"Where do you come from?" asked the Mice. "And what do you know?" They were dreadfully inquisitive. "Tell us about the most beautiful spot on earth. Have you been there? Have you been in the store-room, where cheeses lie on the shelves, and hams hang from the ceiling, where one dances on tallow candles, and goes in thin and comes out fat?"

"I don't know that!" replied the Tree; "but I know the wood, where the sun shines, and where the birds sing."

And then it told all about its youth.

And the little Mice had never heard anything of the kind; and they listened and said,

"What a number of things you have seen! How happy you must have been!"

"I?" said the Fir Tree; and it thought about what it had told. "Yes, those were really quite happy times." But then he told of the Christmas-eve, when he had been hung with sweetmeats and candles.

"Oh!" said the little Mice, "how happy you have been, you old Fir Tree!"

"I'm not old at all," said the Tree. "I only came out of the wood this winter. I'm only rather backward in my growth."

"What splendid stories you can tell!" said the little Mice.

And next night they came with four other little Mice, to hear what the Tree had to relate; and the more it said, the more clearly did it remember everything, and thought, "Those were quite merry days! But they may come again. Klumpey-Dumpey fell down stairs, and yet he married the Princess. Perhaps I may marry a Princess too!" And then the Fir Tree thought of a pretty little birch tree that grew out in the forest: for the Fir Tree, that birch was a real Princess.

"Who's Klumpey-Dumpey?" asked the little Mice.

And then the Fir Tree told the whole story. It could remember every single word: and the little Mice were ready to leap to the very top of the tree with pleasure. Next night a great many more Mice came, and on Sunday two Rats even appeared; but these thought the story was not pretty, and the little Mice were sorry for that, for now they also did not like it so much as before.

"Do you only know one story?" asked the Rats.

"Only that one," replied the Tree. "I heard that on the happiest evening of my life; I did not think then how happy I was."

"That's a very miserable story. Don't you know any about bacon and tallow candles—a store-room story?"

"No," said the Tree.

"Then we'd rather not hear you," said the Rats.

And they went back to their own people. The little Mice at last stayed away also; and then the Tree sighed and said,

"It was very nice when they sat round me, the merry little Mice, and listened when I spoke to them. Now that's past too. But I shall remember to be pleased when they take me out."

But when did that happen? Why, it was one morning that people came and rummaged in the garret: the boxes were put away, and the Tree brought out; they certainly threw him rather roughly on the floor, but a servant dragged him away at once to the stairs, where the daylight shone.

"Now life is beginning again," thought the Tree.

It felt the fresh air and the first sunbeams, and now it was out in the courtyard. Everything passed so quickly that the Tree quite forgot to look at itself, there was so much to look at all round. The courtyard was close to a garden, and here everything was blooming; the roses hung fresh and fragrant over the little paling, the linden trees were in blossom, and the swallows cried, "Quinze-wit! quinze-wit! my husband's come!" But it was not the Fir Tree that they meant.

"Now I shall live!" said the Tree, rejoicingly, and spread its branches far out; but, alas! they were all withered and yellow; and it lay in the corner among nettles and weeds. The tinsel star was still upon it, and shone in the bright sunshine.

In the courtyard a couple of the merry children were playing, who had danced round the tree at Christmas-time, and had

213

rejoiced over it. One of the youngest ran up and tore off the golden star.

"Look what is sticking to the ugly old fir tree," said the child, and he trod upon the branches till they cracked again under his boots.

And the Tree looked at all the blooming flowers and the splendor of the garden, and then looked at itself, and wished it had remained in the dark corner of the garret; it thought of its fresh youth in the wood, of the merry Christmas-eve, and of the little Mice which had listened so pleasantly to the story of Klumpey-Dumpey.

"Past! past!" said the old Tree. "Had I but rejoiced when I could have done so! Past! past!"

And the servant came and chopped the Tree into little pieces; a whole bundle lay there, it blazed brightly under the great brewing copper, and it sighed deeply, and each sigh was like a little shot: and the children who were at play there ran up and seated themselves at the fire, looked into it, and cried, "Puff! puff!" But at each explosion, which was a deep sigh, the Tree thought of a summer day in the woods, or of a winter night there, when the stars beamed; he thought of Christmas-eve and of Klumpey-Dumpey, the only story he had ever heard or knew how to tell; and then the Tree was burned.

The boys played in the garden, and the youngest had on his breast a golden star, which the Tree had worn on its happiest evening. Now that was past, and the Tree's life was past, and the story is past too: past! past!—and that's the way with all stories.

214

LITTLE ROGER'S NIGHT IN THE CHURCH
SUSAN COOLIDGE

The boys and girls had fastened the last sprig of holly upon the walls, and then gone to their homes, leaving the old church silent and deserted. The sun had set in a sky clear and yellow as topaz. Christmas eve had fairly come, and now the moon was rising, a full moon, and all the world looked white in the silver light. Every bough of every tree sparkled with a delicate coating of frost, the pines and cedars were great shapes of dazzling snow, even the ivy on the gothic tower hung a glittering arabesque on the gray wall. Never was there a lovelier night. That light that you see yonder comes from the window of old Andrew, the sexton, and inside sits his grandson, little Roger, eating his supper of porridge. The kitchen is in apple-pie order, chairs and tables have been scrubbed as white as snow, the tins on the dresser shine like silver, the hearth is swept clean, and Grandfather's chair is drawn into the warmest corner. Grandfather is not sitting in it though; he has gone to the church to put the fire in order for the night, lock up the doors, and make all safe.

Grandmother, in her clean stuff gown and apron, is mounted upon a chair to stick a twig of holly on the tall clock in the corner. And now, as she turns round, what a pleasant face she shows us, does she not? Old and wrinkled, to be sure, but so good-natured and gentle that she is prettier than many a young girl even now. Is it any wonder that little Roger there is so fond of her?

Now another bit of holly is wanted on the chimney-piece; and it is while putting this up that the dear old dame gives sign that something has gone wrong. "Ts, ts, ts,—deary me!"

"What's the matter, Granny?" said Roger.

"Why, Roger," replied Granny, carefully dismounting from her chair, "look here, Grandfather has gone off and forgot his keys. He took 'em from the door this morning, because last year some of the young folks let 'em drop in the snow, and had a sad time hunting for them. He knew they would be in and out all day, so he just opened the door and brought the keys home. Deary me! it's a cold night for old bones to be out of doors. Would'st be afeard, little 'un, to run up with them?"

"Not a bit," said Roger, stoutly, as he crammed the last spoonful of porridge in his mouth, and seized hat and mittens from the table. "I'll take 'em down in a minute. Granny, and then run home. Mother'll want me in the morning, likely."

For Roger's parents lived in a cottage near the old people, and the boy often said that he had two homes, and belonged half in one and half in the other, and the small press-bed in Granny's loft seemed as much his own as the cot in the corner of his mother's sleeping-room, and was occupied almost as often. So, after a good-night hug from Granny, off he ran. The church was near, and the moon light as day, so he never thought of being afraid, not even when, as he brushed by the dark tower, something stirred overhead, and a long, melancholy cry came shuddering from the ivy. Roger knew the owls in the belfry well, and now he called out to them cheerily: "To-whit-whit-whoo!"

"Whoo-whoo-whit!" answered the owls, startled by the cry. Roger could hear them fluttering in the nest.

The church-door stood ajar, and he peeped in. The glow from the open door of the stove showed Grandfather's figure, red and warm, stooping to cover the fire with ashes for the night.

He was so busy he never knew the boy was there till he got close to him and jingled the keys in his ear; but after one start he laughed, well pleased.

"I but just missed them," he said. "Thou'rt a good boy to fetch them up. Art going home with me to-night?"

"No, I'm to sleep at my mother's," said Roger, "but I'll wait and walk with you, Grandfather." So he slipped into a pew, and sat down till the work should be finished, and they ready to go; and as he looked up he saw all at once how beautiful the old church was looking.

The moon outside was streaming in so brightly, that you hardly missed the sun, Roger could see distinctly way up to the carved beams of the roof, and trace the figures on the great arched

216

windows over the altar, whose colors had so often dazzled him on Sundays. The colors were soft and dim now, but the figures were there. Roger could see them plainly,—the sitting figure of the Lord Christ, with St. Matthew and two other apostles, and the fisher-lad with his basket of fish. He had often asked Granny to read him the story.

That gleam at the further end of the nave came from the organ-loft, where the moonbeams had found out the great brass pipes, and were playing all manner of tricks with them. Almost the red of the holly-berries could be seen, and every pointed ivy-leaf and spike of evergreen in the wreathings of the windows stood out in bold relief against the shining panes. With this beautiful whiteness the red glow of the fire blended, and flooded the chancel with a lovely pink light, in which shone the gilded letters on the commandment-tables, and the brasses of the tablets on the walls. It was a wonderful thing to see.

To study the roof better, Roger thought he would lie flat on the cushion awhile, and look straight up. So he arranged himself comfortably, and somehow—it *will* happen, even when we are full of enjoyment and pleasure—his eyes shut, and the first thing he knew he was rubbing them open again, only a minute afterward, as it seemed; but Grandfather was gone. There was the stove closed for the night, and the great door at the end of the aisle was shut. He jumped up in a fright, as you can imagine, and ran to see, and shook it hard. No: it was locked, and poor Roger was fastened in for the night.

He understood it all in a moment. The tall pew had hidden him from sight. Grandfather had thought him gone home; his mother would ever doubt that he was safe at the other cottage; no one would miss him, and there was no chance of being let out before morning.

He was only six years old, so no wonder that at first he felt choked and frightened, and inclined to cry. But he was a brave lad, and that idea soon left him. He began to think that he was not badly off, after all,—the church was warm, the pew-cushion as soft as his bed. No one could get in to harm him. In fact, after the first moment, there was something so exciting and adventurous in the idea of spending the night in such a place, that he was almost glad the accident had happened. So he went back to the pew, and tried to go to sleep again.

That was not so easy. Did you ever get thoroughly waked up in the night by a sudden fright? Do you remember how your eyes wouldn't stay shut afterward, even when you closed them tight, but jerked open almost against your will, as if a string was fastened to them and some one was twitching it? Just so poor Roger felt. He lay still and kept himself quiet for a moment, and then some little noise would come, and his heart beat and his eyes be wide open in a minute. It was a coal dropping from the fire, or a slight crack on the frosty panes: once a little mouse crept out from the chancel, glaring shyly about with his bright eyes, nibbled a moment at a leaf on the carpet and then crept back again. No other living thing disturbed the quiet.

He had heard the clock strike eleven a long time since, and was lying with eyes half shut, gazing at the red fire-grate, and feeling at last a little drowsy, when all at once a strange rush and thrill seemed to come to him in the air, like a cool clear wind blowing through the church, and in one minute he was wide awake and sitting upright, with ears strained to catch some sound afar off. It was too distant and faint for ordinary sense, but a new and sharper power of hearing seemed given him. Little voices were speaking high in the air, outside the church,—very odd ones, like birds' notes, and yet the words were plain. He listened and listened, and made out at last that it was the owls in the tower talking together.

"Hoo, hoo, why don't you lie still there?" said one.

"Whit-whoo-whit," said the other, "I can't. I know what is coming too well for that."

"What is coming,—what, what?" said two voices together.

"Ah! you'll see soon," replied the first. "The elves are coming, the hateful Christmas elves. You'll not get a wink of sleep to-night."

"Why not? What will they do to us?" chirped the young ones.

218

"You'll see," hooted the old owl. "You'll see! They'll pull your tails, and tickle your feathers, and prick you with thorns. I know them, the tricksy, troublesome things! I've been here many a long year. You were only hatched last summer. To-whoo, to-whoo!"

Just at this moment the church-clock began to strike twelve. At the first clang the owls ceased to hoot, and Roger listened to the deep notes, almost awe-struck, as they sounded one by one. He knew the voice of the clock well, but it never before sounded so loud or so solemn: five—six—seven—eight—nine—ten—eleven—twelve. It was Christmas Day.

As the last echo died away, a new sound took its place. From afar off came the babble of tiny voices drawing nearer. Anything so gay and charming was never dreamed of before,—half a laugh, half a song, the tones blended into an enchanting peal, like bells on a frolic. Above the old tower the sounds clustered and increased,—then a long, distressed cry came from the owl, and a bubbling laugh floated in on the wind. Roger could not stand it. Wild to see, he flew to the window, and tried to stretch his neck in such a way as to catch what was going on above; but it was a vain attempt, and just then the church-bells began to ring all together, a chime, a Christmas chime, only the sounds were infinitely small, as if baby hands had laid hold on the ropes. But his sharpened senses brought every note and change to Roger's ears, and they were so merry and so lovely that he felt he must get nearer or die; and almost before he knew it he was climbing the dark belfry-stairs as fast as his feet could carry him, never thinking of fear or darkness, only of the elfin bells which were pealing overhead.

Up, up, through the long slits in the tower the moon could be seen sailing in the cold, clear blue. Higher, higher,—at last he gained the belfry. There hung the four great bells, but nobody was pulling at their heavy ropes. On each iron tongue was perched a fay; on the chains which suspended them clustered others, all keeping time by the swaying of their bodies as they swung to and fro, just grazing either side, and bringing forth a

219

clear, delicate stroke, sweet as laughter,—just loud enough for fairy ears.

Through the windows the crowd of floating fays could be seen whirling about in the moonlight like glittering gossamer. They floated in and out of the tower, they mounted the great bells and sat atop in swarms, they chased and pushed each other, playing all sorts of pranks. Below, others were attacking the owl's nest. Roger could hear their hoots and grunts and the gleeful laughter of the elves. The moon made the tower light as noon; all the time the elves sang or talked,—which, he could not tell; there were words, but all so blent with laughs and mirthful trills that it was nothing less than music.

To and fro, to and fro, keeping time to a fairy rhythm, they swayed in unison with the tiny peal they rang. Little quarrels arose. Once Roger watched an elf trying to mount the clapper, and whenever he neared the top a mischievous comrade pushed him off again. Then the elf pouted, and, flying away, he returned with a holly-leaf. Small as it was, it curled over his head like a huge umbrella. With the spiky point he slyly pricked the elf above; and he, taken by surprise, lost his hold, and came tumbling down, while the other danced for glee and clapped his hands mockingly. Pretty soon, however, all was made up again,—they kissed and were friends,—and Roger saw them perched opposite each other, and moving to and fro like children in a swing.

How long the pretty sight lasted he could not tell. So fearful was he of marring the sport that he never stirred a finger; but all at once there came a strain of music in the air, solemn, and sweeter than ever mortal heard before. In a moment the elves left their sports; they clustered like bees together in the window, and then flew from the tower in one sparkling drift, and were gone, leaving Roger alone, and the owls hooting below in the ivy.

And then he felt afraid,—which he had not been as long as the fays were there,—and down he ran in a fright over the stone steps of the stairs, and entered the church again. The red glow

220

of the fire was grateful to him, for he was shivering with cold and excitement; but hardly had he regained his old seat, when, lo! a great marvel came to pass. The wide window over the altar swung open, and a train of angels slowly floated through. How he knew them to be angels, Roger could not have told; but that they were, he was sure,—Christmas angels, with faces of calm, glorious beauty, and robes as white as snow. Over the altar they hovered, and a wonderful song rose and filled the church—no bird's strain was ever half so sweet. The words were few, but again and again and again they came: "Glory to God in the highest, on earth peace, good-will to men!"

Roger knew the oft-repeated words,—they were those of the great evergreen motto which overarched the chancel; but I think he never forgot the beautiful meaning they seemed to bear as the angels sang them over and over. It was so wondrous sweet that he could not feel afraid,—he could only gaze and gaze, and hold his breath lest he should lose a note.

And the song rang on, clear and triumphant, even as the white-robed choir parted and floated like soft summer clouds to and fro in the church, pausing ever and anon as in blessing. They touched the leaves of the Christmas green as they passed; they hung over the organ and brushed the keys with their wings; a long time they clustered above the benches of the poor, as if to leave a fragrance in the air; and then they rested before a tablet which had been put up but a few months before, and which bore the name of the rector's eldest son, and the dates of his birth and death. Roger had been told of this brave lad, and how he had lost his life in plunging from his ship to save the drowning child of an emigrant; and now the angel-song seemed sweeter than ever, as over and again they chanted, "Good-will to men,—good-will to men."

At last one of the white-winged ones left the others, and hovered awhile above the Squire's pew, near which our little boy was hidden. A prayer-book lay open on the rail, and over this the fair angel bent as in benediction. A girl had sat there once,—the Squire's only daughter. Roger remembered her well, and the mourning of the whole parish when, only a twelvemonth ago, the lovely child had been buried from their sight; and now, as he timidly glanced into the glorious face above him, it seemed to him to have the same look, only so ineffably beautiful that he closed his dazzled eyes to shut out the vision and the light that shone from the white wings,—only for a moment, then he opened them again, as a gentle rustling filled the air, and he saw the bending figure stoop, leave a kiss or a blessing on the pages of the open book, and then glide away with the others. Again the group hovered above the altar,—louder and clearer rose the triumphant strain, and, noiseless as a cloud, the snowy train floated to the window. For one moment their figures could be seen against the sky, then the song died away,—they were gone, and Roger saw them no more.

And now the light of dawn began to creep into the windows, twittering sounds showed the birds awakening outside, and a pink streak appeared in the sky. Too much rapt by his vision to feel impatience, the boy sat and waited; and by and by a jingling in the lock showed Grandfather at hand,—the door opened, and he came in.

You can guess his surprise when his little grandson flew to meet him with his wonderful story. As for the story, he pooh-poohed *that*,—sleeping in such a strange place might well bring about a queer dream, he said; but he took the boy home to the cottage, and Granny, full of wonderment and sympathy, speedily prepared a breakfast for her darling after his adventure. But, even with his mouth full of scalding bread and milk, Roger would go on telling of angels and fairies, and the owls' talk in their nest, till both grandparents began to think him bewitched.

Perhaps he was, for to this day he persists in the story. And though the villagers that morning exclaimed that at no time had their old church, in its Christmas dress, looked so beautiful before, and though the organ sent forth a rarer, sweeter music than fingers had ever drawn from it, still nobody believed a

222

word of it. And though the poor mother, kneeling in her lonely pew, and missing her darling from beside her, felt a strange peace and patience enter her heart, and came away calmed and blessed, still no one listened to the story. "Roger had dreamed it all," they said; and perhaps he had,—only the owls knew.

MR. BLUFFS EXPERIENCES OF HOLIDAYS
OLIVER BELL BUNCE

"I hate holidays," said Bachelor Bluff to me, with some little irritation, on a Christmas a few years ago. Then he paused an instant, after which he resumed: "I don't mean to say that I hate to see people enjoying themselves. But I hate holidays, nevertheless, because to me they are always the dreariest and saddest days of the year. I shudder at the name of holiday. I dread the approach of one, and thank Heaven when it is over. I pass through, on a holiday, the most horrible sensations, the bitterest feelings, the most oppressive melancholy; in fact, I am not myself at holiday-times."

"Very strange," I ventured to interpose.

"A plague on it!" said he, almost with violence. "I'm not inhuman. I don't wish anybody harm. I'm glad people can enjoy themselves. But I hate holidays all the same. You see, this is the reason: I am a bachelor; I am without kin; I am in a place that did not know me at birth. And so, when holidays come around, there is no place anywhere for me. I have friends, of course; I don't think I've been a very sulky, shut-in, reticent fellow; and there is many a board that has a place for me—but not at Christmas-time. At Christmas, the dinner is a family gathering; and I've no family. There is such a gathering of kindred on this occasion, such a reunion of family folk, that there is no place for a friend, even if the friend be liked. Christmas, with all its kindliness and charity and good-will, is, after all, deuced selfish. Each little set gathers within its own circle; and people like me, with no particular circle, are left in the lurch. So you see, on the day of all the days in the year that my heart pines for good cheer, I'm without an invitation.

"Oh, it's because I pine for good cheer," said the bachelor, sharply, interrupting my attempt to speak, "that I hate holidays. If I were an infernally selfish fellow, I wouldn't hate holidays. I'd go off and have some fun all to myself, somewhere or somehow. But, you see, I hate to be in the dark when all the rest of the world is in light. I hate holidays, because I ought to be merry and happy on holidays, and can't.

"Don't tell me," he cried, stopping the word that was on my lips; "I tell you, I hate holidays. The shops look merry, do they, with their bright toys and their green branches? The pantomime is crowded with merry hearts, is it? The circus and the show are brimful of fun and laughter, are they? Well, they all make me miserable. I haven't any pretty-faced girls or bright-eyed boys to take to the circus or the show, and all the nice girls and fine boys of my acquaintance have their uncles or their grand-dads or their cousins to take them to those places; so, if I go, I must go alone. But I don't go. I can't bear the chill of seeing everybody happy, and knowing myself so lonely and desolate. Confound it, sir, I've too much heart to be happy under such circumstances! I'm too humane, sir! And the result is, I hate holidays. It's miserable to be out, and yet I can't stay at home, for I get thinking of Christmases past. I can't read—the shadow of my heart makes it impossible. I can't walk—for I see nothing but pictures through the bright windows, and happy groups of pleasure-seekers. The fact is, I've nothing to do but to hate holidays.—But will you not dine with me?"

Of course, I had to plead engagement with my own family circle, and I couldn't quite invite Mr. Bluff home *that* day, when Cousin Charles and his wife, and Sister Susan and her daughter and three of my wife's kin, had come in from the country, all to make a merry Christmas with us. I felt sorry, but it was quite impossible, so I wished Mr. Bluff a "merry Christmas," and hurried homeward through the cold and nipping air.

I did not meet Bachelor Bluff again until a week after Christmas of the next year, when I learned some strange particulars of what occurred to him after our parting on the occasion just described. I will let Bachelor Bluff tell his adventure for himself:

"I went to church," said he, "and was as sad there as everywhere else. Of course, the evergreens were pretty, and the music fine; but all around me were happy groups of people, who could scarcely keep down *merry* Christmas long enough to

225

do reverence to *sacred* Christmas. And nobody was alone but me. Every happy paterfamilias in his pew tantalized me, and the whole atmosphere of the place seemed so much better suited to every one else than me that I came away hating holidays worse than ever. Then I went to the play, and sat down in a box all alone by myself. Everybody seemed on the best of terms with everybody else, and jokes and banter passed from one to another with the most good-natured freedom. Everybody but me was in a little group of friends. I was the only person in the whole theater that was alone. And then there was such clapping of hands, and roars of laughter, and shouts of delight at all the fun going on upon the stage, all of which was rendered doubly enjoyable by everybody having somebody with whom to share and interchange the pleasure, that my loneliness got simply unbearable, and I hated holidays infinitely worse than ever.
"By five o'clock the holiday became so intolerable that I said I'd go and get a dinner. The best dinner the town could provide. A sumptuous dinner. A sumptuous dinner for one. A dinner with many courses, with wines of the finest brands, with bright lights, with a cheerful fire, with every condition of comfort—and I'd see if I couldn't for once extract a little pleasure out of a holiday!
"The handsome dining-room at the club looked bright, but it was empty. Who dines at this club on Christmas but lonely bachelors? There was a flutter of surprise when I ordered a dinner, and the few attendants were, no doubt, glad of something to break the monotony of the hours.
"My dinner was well served. The spacious room looked lonely; but the white, snowy cloths, the rich window-hangings, the warm tints of the walls, the sparkle of the fire in the steel grate, gave the room an air of elegance and cheerfulness; and then the table at which I dined was close to the window, and through the partly-drawn curtains were visible centers of lonely, cold streets, with bright lights from many a window, it is true, but there was a storm, and snow began whirling through the street. I let my imagination paint the streets as cold and dreary as it

would, just to extract a little pleasure by way of contrast from the brilliant room of which I was apparently sole master.

"I dined well, and recalled in fancy old, youthful Christmases, and pledged mentally many an old friend, and my melancholy was mellowing into a low, sad undertone, when, just as I was raising a glass of wine to my lips, I was startled by a picture at the window-pane. It was a pale, wild, haggard face, in a great cloud of black hair, pressed against the glass. As I looked, it vanished. With a strange thrill at my heart, which my lips mocked with a derisive sneer, I finished the wine and set down the glass. It was, of course, only a beggar-girl that had crept up to the window and stole a glance at the bright scene within; but still the pale face troubled me a little, and threw a fresh shadow on my heart. I filled my glass once more with wine, and was again about to drink, when the face reappeared at the window. It was so white, so thin, with eyes so large, wild, and hungry-looking, and the black, unkempt hair, into which the snow had drifted, formed so strange and weird a frame to the picture, that I was fairly startled. Replacing, untasted, the liquor on the table, I rose and went close to the pane. The face had vanished, and I could see no object within many feet of the window. The storm had increased, and the snow was driving in wild gusts through the streets, which were empty, save here and there a hurrying wayfarer. The whole scene was cold, wild, and desolate, and I could not repress a keen thrill of sympathy for the child, whoever it was, whose only Christmas was to watch, in cold and storm, the rich banquet ungratefully enjoyed by the lonely bachelor. I resumed my place at the table; but the dinner was finished, and the wine had no further relish. I was haunted by the vision at the window, and began, with an unreasonable irritation at the interruption, to repeat with fresh warmth my detestation of holidays. One couldn't even dine alone on a holiday with any sort of comfort, I declared. On holidays one was tormented by too much pleasure on one side, and too much misery on the other. And then, I said, hunting for justification of my dislike of the day, 'How many other people are, like me, made miserable by seeing the fullness of enjoyment others possessed!

"Oh, yes, I know," sarcastically replied the bachelor to a comment of mine; "of course, all magnanimous, generous, and noble-souled people delight in seeing other people made happy, and are quite content to accept this vicarious felicity. But I, you see, and this dear little girl—"

"Dear little girl!"

"Oh, I forgot," said Bachelor Bluff, blushing a little, in spite of a desperate effort not to do so, "I didn't tell you. Well, it was so absurd! I kept thinking, thinking of the pale, haggard, lonely little girl on the cold and desolate side of the window-pane, and the over-fed, discontented, lonely old bachelor on the splendid side of the window-pane; and I didn't get much happier thinking about it, I can assure you. I drank glass after glass of the wine—not that I enjoyed its flavor any more, but mechanically, as it were, and with a sort of hope thereby to drown unpleasant reminders. I tried to attribute my annoyance in the matter to holidays, and so denounced them more vehemently than ever. I rose once in a while and went to the window, but could see no one to whom the pale face could have belonged.

"At last, in no very amiable mood, I got up, put on my wrappers, and went out; and the first thing I did was to run against a small figure crouching in the doorway. A face looked up quickly at the rough encounter, and I saw the pale features of the window-pane. I was very irritated and angry, and spoke harshly; and then, all at once, I am sure I don't know how it happened, but it flashed upon me that I, of all men, had no right to utter a harsh word to one oppressed with so wretched a Christmas as this poor creature was. I couldn't say another word, but began feeling in my pocket for some money, and then I asked a question or two, and then I don't quite know how it came about—isn't it very warm here?" exclaimed Bachelor Bluff, rising and walking about, and wiping the perspiration from his brow.

"Well, you see," he resumed nervously, "it was very absurd, but I did believe the girl's story—the old story, you know, of privation and suffering, and all that—and just thought I'd go home with the brat and see if what she said was all true. And then I remembered that all the shops were closed, and not a purchase could be made. I went back and persuaded the steward to put up for me a hamper of provisions, which the half-wild little youngster helped me carry through the snow, dancing with delight all the way.—And isn't this enough?"

"Not a bit, Mr. Bluff. I must have the whole story."

"I declare," said Bachelor Bluff, "there's no whole story to tell. A widow with children in great need, that was what I found; and they had a feast that night, and a little money to buy them a load of wood and a garment or two the next day; and they were all so bright, and so merry, and so thankful, and so good, that, when I got home that night, I was mightily amazed that, instead of going to bed sour at holidays, I was in a state of great contentment in regard to holidays. In fact, I was really merry. I whistled. I sang. I do believe I cut a caper. The poor wretches I had left had been so merry over their unlooked-for Christmas banquet that their spirits infected mine.

"And then I got thinking again. Of course, holidays had been miserable to me, I said. What right had a well-to-do, lonely old bachelor hovering wistfully in the vicinity of happy circles, when all about there were so many people as lonely as he, and yet oppressed with want? 'Good gracious!' I exclaimed, 'to think of a man complaining of loneliness with thousands of wretches yearning for his help and comfort, with endless opportunities for work and company, with hundreds of pleasant and delightful things to do! Just to think of it!' It put me in a great fury at myself to think of it. I tried pretty hard to escape from myself and began inventing excuses and all that sort of thing, but I rigidly forced myself to look squarely at my own conduct. And then I reconciled my conscience by declaring that, if ever after that day I hated a holiday again, might my holidays end at once and forever!

"Did I go and see my *protégés* again? What a question! Why—well, no matter. If the widow is comfortable now, it is because she has found a way to earn without difficulty enough for her few wants. That's no fault of mine. I would have done more for her, but she wouldn't let me. But just let me tell you about New Year's—the New-Year's-day that followed the Christmas I've been describing. It was lucky for me there was another holiday only a week off. Bless you! I had so much to do that day that I was completely bewildered, and the hours weren't half long enough. I did make a few social calls, but then I hurried them over; and then hastened to my little girl, whose face had already caught a touch of color; and she, looking quite handsome in her new frock and her ribbons, took me to other poor folk, and—well, that's about the whole story.

"Oh, as to the next Christmas. Well, I didn't dine alone, as you may guess. It was up three stairs, that's true, and there was none of that elegance that marked the dinner of the year before; but it was merry, and happy, and bright; it was a generous, honest, hearty, Christmas dinner, that it was, although I do wish the widow hadn't talked so much about the mysterious way a turkey had been left at her door the night before. And Molly—that's the little girl—and I had a rousing appetite. We went to church early; then we had been down to the Five Points to carry the poor outcasts there something for their Christmas dinner; in fact, we had done wonders of work, and Molly was in high spirits, and so the Christmas dinner was a great success.

"Dear me, sir, no! Just as you say. Holidays are not in the least wearisome any more. Plague on it! When a man tells me now that he hates holidays, I find myself getting very wroth. I pin him by the button-hole at once, and tell him my experience. The fact is, if I were at dinner on a holiday, and anybody should ask me for a sentiment, I should say, God bless all holidays!"

SANTA CLAUS AT SIMPSON'S BAR
BRET HARTE

It was nearly midnight when the festivities were interrupted.

"Hush!" said Dick Bullen, holding up his hand. It was the querulous voice of Johnny from his adjacent closet: "Oh, dad!"

The Old Man arose hurriedly and disappeared in the closet. Presently he reappeared. "His rheumatiz is coming on agin bad," he explained, "and he wants rubbin'." He lifted the demijohn of whiskey from the table and shook it. It was empty. Dick Bullen put down his tin cup with an embarrassed laugh. So did the others. The Old Man examined their contents, and said hopefully, "I reckon that's enough; he don't need much. You hold on, all o' you, for a spell, and I'll be back;" and vanished in the closet with an old flannel shirt and the whiskey. The door closed but imperfectly, and the following dialogue was distinctly audible:—

"Now, sonny, whar does she ache worst?"

"Sometimes over yar and sometimes under yer; but it's most powerful from yer to yer. Rub yer, dad."

A silence seemed to indicate a brisk rubbing. Then Johnny:—

"Hevin' a good time out yar, dad?"

"Yes, sonny."

"Tomorrer's Chrismiss,—ain't it?"

"Yes, sonny. How does she feel now?"

"Better. Rub a little furder down. Wot's Chrismiss, anyway? Wot's it all about?"

"Oh, it's a day."

This exhaustive definition was apparently satisfactory, for there was a silent interval of rubbing. Presently Johnny again:—

"Mar sez that everywhere else but yer everybody gives things to everybody Chrismiss, and then she jist waded inter you. She sez thar's a man they call Sandy Claws, not a white man, you know, but a kind o' Chinemin, comes down the chimbley night afore Chrismiss and gives things to chillern,—boys like me. Puts 'em in their butes! Thet's what she tried to play upon me. Easy, now, pop, whar are you rubbin' to,—thet's a mile from the place. She

231

jest made that up, didn't she, jest to aggrewate me and you? Don't rub thar—Why, dad!"

In the great quiet that seemed to have fallen upon the house the sigh of the near pines and the drip of leaves without was very distinct. Johnny's voice, too, was lowered as he went on: "Don't you take on now, for I'm gettin' all right fast. Wot's the boys doin' out thar?"

The Old Man partly opened the door and peered through. His guests were sitting there sociably enough, and there were a few silver coins and a lean buckskin purse on the table. "Bettin' on suthin',—some little game or 'nother. They're all right," he replied to Johnny, and recommenced his rubbing.

"I'd like to take a hand and win some money," said Johnny reflectively, after a pause.

The Old Man glibly repeated what was evidently a familiar formula, that if Johnny would wait until he struck it rich in the tunnel, he'd have lots of money, etc., etc.

"Yes," said Johnny, "but you don't. And whether you strike it or I win it, it's about the same. It's all luck. But it's mighty cur'o's about Chrismiss,—ain't it? Why do they call it Chrismiss?"

Perhaps from some instinctive deference to the overhearing of his guests, or from some vague sense of incongruity, the Old Man's reply was so low as to be inaudible beyond the room.

"Yes," said Johnny, with some slight abatement of interest, "I've heerd o' him before. Thar, that'll do dad. I don't ache near so bad as I did. Now wrap me tight in this yer blanket. So. Now," he added in a muffled whisper, "sit down yer by me till I go asleep."

To assure himself of obedience he disengaged one hand from the blanket, and, grasping his father's sleeve, again composed himself to rest.

For some moments the Old Man waited patiently. Then the unwonted stillness of the house excited his curiosity, and without moving from the bed he cautiously opened the door with his disengaged hand, and looked into the main room. To his infinite surprise it was dark and deserted. But even then a smoldering log on the hearth broke, and by the upspringing blaze he saw the figure of Dick Bullen sitting by the dying embers.

"Hello!"

Dick started, rose, and came somewhat unsteadily toward him. "Whar's the boys?" said the Old Man.

"Gone up the canon on a little pasear. They're coming back for me in a minit. I'm waitin' round for 'em. What are you starin' at, Old Man?" he added, with a forced laugh; "do you think I'm drunk?"

The Old Man might have been pardoned the supposition, for Dick's eyes were humid and his face flushed. He loitered and lounged back to the chimney, yawned, shook himself, buttoned up his coat and laughed. "Liquor ain't so plenty as that, Old Man. Now don't you git up," he continued, as the Old Man made a movement to release his sleeve from Johnny's hand. "Don't you mind manners. Sit jest whar you be; I'm goin' in a jiffy. Thar, that's them now."

There was a low tap at the door. Dick Bullen opened it quickly, nodded "Good-night" to his host, and disappeared. The Old Man would have followed him but for the hand that still unconsciously grasped his sleeve. He could have easily disengaged it; it was small, weak and emaciated. But perhaps because it was small, weak and emaciated he changed his mind, and, drawing his chair closer to the bed, rested his head upon it. In this defenceless attitude the potency of his earlier potations surprised him. The room flickered and faded before his eyes, reappeared, faded again, went out, and left him—asleep.

Meantime Dick Bullen, closing the door, confronted his companions. "Are you ready?" said Staples. "Ready," said Dick; "what's the time?" "Past twelve," was the reply; "can you make it?—it's nigh on fifty miles, the round trip hither and yon." "I reckon," returned Dick shortly. "Whar's the mare?" "Bill and Jack's holdin' her at the crossin'." "Let 'em hold on a minit longer," said Dick.

He turned and reentered the house softly. By the light of the guttering candle and dying fire he saw that the door of the little room was open. He stepped toward it on tiptoe and looked in. The Old Man had fallen back in his chair, snoring, his helpless feet thrust out in a line with his collapsed shoulders, and his hat pulled over his eyes. Beside him, on a narrow wooden bedstead, lay Johnny, muffled tightly in a blanket that hid all save a strip of forehead and a few curls damp with perspiration. Dick Bullen made a step forward, hesitated, and glanced over his shoulder into the deserted room. Everything was quiet. With a sudden resolution he parted his huge mustaches with both hands, and stooped over the sleeping boy. But even as he did so a mischievous blast, lying in wait, swooped down the chimney, rekindled the hearth, and lit up the room with a shameless glow, from which Dick fled in bashful terror.

His companions were already waiting for him at the crossing. Two of them were struggling in the darkness with some strange misshapen bulk, which as Dick came nearer took the semblance of a great yellow horse.

It was the mare. She was not a pretty picture. From her Roman nose to her rising haunches, from her arched spine hidden by the stiff *machillas* of a Mexican saddle, to her thick, straight, bony legs, there was not a line of equine grace. In her half blind but wholly vicious white eyes, in her protruding under-lip, in her monstrous color, there was nothing but ugliness and vice.

"Now, then," said Staples, "stand cl'ar of her heels, boy, and up with you. Don't miss your first holt of her mane, and mind ye get your off stirrup quick. Ready!"

There was a leap, a scrambling, a bound, a wild retreat of the crowd, a circle of flying hoofs, two springless leaps that jarred the earth, a rapid play and jingle of spurs, a plunge, and then the voice of Dick somewhere in the darkness. "All right!"

"Don't take the lower road back onless you're pushed hard for time! Don't hold her in down hill. We'll be at the ford at five. G'lang! Hoopa! Mula! GO!"

A splash, a spark struck from the ledge in the road, a clatter in the rocky cut beyond, and Dick was gone.

- - - - -

Sing, O Muse, the ride of Richard Bullen! Sing, O Muse, of chivalrous men! the sacred quest, the doughty deeds, the battery of low churls, the fearsome ride and gruesome perils of the Flower of Simpson's Bar! Alack! she is dainty, this Muse! She will have none of this bucking brute and swaggering, ragged rider, and I must fain follow him in prose, afoot!

It was one o'clock, and yet he had only gained Rattlesnake Hill. For in that time Jovita had rehearsed to him all her imperfections and practised all her vices. Thrice had she stumbled. Twice had she thrown up her Roman nose in a straight line with the reins, and, resisting bit and spur, struck out madly across country. Twice had she reared, and, rearing, fallen backward; and twice had the agile Dick, unharmed, regained his seat before she found her vicious legs again. And a mile beyond them, at the foot of a long hill, was Rattlesnake Creek. Dick knew that here was the crucial test of his ability to perform his enterprise, set his teeth grimly, put his knees well into her flanks, and changed his defensive tactics to brisk aggression. Bullied and maddened, Jovita began the descent of the hill. Here the artful Richard pretended to hold her in with ostentatious objurgation and well-feigned cries of alarm. It is unnecessary to add that Jovita instantly ran away. Nor need I state the time made in the descent; it is written in the chronicles of Simpson's Bar. Enough that in another moment, as it seemed to Dick, she was splashing on the overflowed banks of Rattlesnake Creek. As Dick expected, the momentum she had acquired carried her beyond the point of balking, and, holding her well together for a mighty leap, they dashed into the middle of the swiftly flowing current. A few moments of kicking, wading, and swimming, and Dick drew a long breath on the opposite bank.

The road from Rattlesnake Creek to Red Mountain was tolerably level. Either the plunge into Rattlesnake Creek had dampened her baleful fire, or the art which led to it had shown her the superior wickedness of her rider, for Jovita no longer wasted her surplus energy in wanton conceits. Once she bucked, but it

235

was from force of habit; once she shied, but it was from a new, freshly-painted meeting-house at the crossing of the country road. Hollows, ditches, gravelly deposits, patches of freshly-springing grasses, flew from beneath her rattling hoofs. She began to smell unpleasantly, once or twice she coughed slightly, but there was no abatement of her strength or speed. By two o'clock he had passed Red Mountain and begun the descent to the plain. Ten minutes later the driver of the fast Pioneer coach was overtaken and passed by a "man on a Pinto hoss,"—an event sufficiently notable for remark. At half past two Dick rose in his stirrups with a great shout. Stars were glittering through the rifted clouds, and beyond him, out of the plain, rose two spires, a flagstaff, and a straggling line of black objects. Dick jingled his spurs and swung his *riata*, Jovita bounded forward, and in another moment they swept into Tuttleville, and drew up before the wooden piazza of "The Hotel of All Nations." What transpired that night at Tuttleville is not strictly a part of this record. Briefly I may state, however, that after Jovita had been handed over to a sleepy ostler, whom she at once kicked into unpleasant consciousness, Dick sallied out with the barkeeper for a tour of the sleeping town. Lights still gleamed from a few saloons and gambling houses; but, avoiding these, they stopped before several closed shops, and by persistent tapping and judicious outcry roused the proprietors from their beds, and made them unbar the doors of their magazines and expose their wares. Sometimes they were met by curses, but oftener by interest and some concern in their needs. It was three o'clock before this pleasantry was given over, and with a small waterproof bag of India rubber strapped on his shoulders Dick returned to the hotel. And then he sprang to the saddle, and dashed down the lonely street and out into the lonelier plain, where presently the lights, the black line of houses, the spires, and the flagstaff sank into the earth behind him again and were lost in the distance.

The storm had cleared away, the air was brisk and cold, the outlines of adjacent landmarks were distinct, but it was half-past four before Dick reached the meeting-house and the crossing of the country road. To avoid the rising grade he had taken a longer and more circuitous road, in whose viscid mud Jovita sank fetlock deep at every bound. It was a poor preparation for a steady ascent of five miles more; but Jovita, gathering her legs under her, took it with her usual blind, unreasoning fury, and a half hour later reached the long level that led to Rattlesnake Creek. Another half hour would bring him to the Creek. He threw the reins lightly upon the neck of the mare, chirruped to her, and began to sing.

Suddenly Jovita shied with a bound that would have unseated a less practised rider. Hanging to her rein was a figure that had leaped from the bank, and at the same time from the road before her arose a shadowy horse and rider. "Throw up your hands," commanded the second apparition, with an oath.

Dick felt the mare tremble, quiver, and apparently sink under him. He knew what it meant, and was prepared.

"Stand aside, Jack Simpson. I know you, you d——d thief! Let me pass, or—"

He did not finish the sentence. Jovita rose straight in the air with a terrific bound, throwing the figure from her bit with a single shake of her vicious head, and charged with deadly malevolence down on the impediment before her. An oath, a pistol-shot, horse and highwayman rolled over in the road, and the next moment Jovita was a hundred yards away. But the good right arm of her rider, shattered by a bullet, dropped helplessly at his side.

Without slacking his speed he lifted the reins to his left hand. But a few moments later he was obliged to halt and tighten the saddle-girths that had slipped in the onset. This in his crippled condition took some time. He had no fear of pursuit, but, looking up, he saw that the eastern stars were already paling, and that the distant peaks had lost their ghostly whiteness, and now stood out blackly against a lighter sky. Day was upon him. Then completely absorbed in a single idea, he forgot the pain of his wound, and, mounting again, dashed on towards

Rattlesnake Creek. But now Jovita's breath came broken by gasps, Dick reeled in his saddle, and brighter and brighter grew the sky.

Ride, Richard; run, Jovita; linger, O day!

For the last few rods there was a roaring in his ears. Was it exhaustion from a loss of blood, or what? He was dazed and giddy as he swept down the hill, and did not recognize his surroundings. Had he taken the wrong road, or was this Rattlesnake Creek?

It was. But the brawling creek he had swam a few hours before had risen, more than doubled its volume, and now rolled a swift and resistless river between him and Rattlesnake Hill. For the first time that night Richard's heart sank within him. The river, the mountain, the quickening east, swam before his eyes. He shut them to recover his self-control. In that brief interval, by some fantastic mental process, the little room at Simpson's Bar and the figures of the sleeping father and son rose upon him. He opened his eyes wildly, cast off his coat, pistol, boots, and saddle, bound his precious pack tightly to his shoulders, grasped the bare flanks of Jovita with his bared knees, and with a shout dashed into the yellow water. A cry arose from the opposite bank as the head of a man and horse struggled for a few moments against the battling current, and then were swept away amidst uprooted trees and whirling driftwood.

- - - - -

The Old man started and woke. The fire on the hearth was dead, the candle in the outer room flickering in its socket, and somebody was rapping at the door. He opened it, but fell back with a cry before the dripping, half-naked figure that reeled against the doorpost.

"Dick?"

"Hush! Is he awake yet?"

"No; but Dick—"

"Dry up, you old fool! Get me some whiskey, quick!" The Old Man flew, and returned with—an empty bottle! Dick would have sworn, but his strength was not equal to the occasion. He

238

staggered, caught at the handle of the door, and motioned to the Old Man.

"Thar's suthin' in my pack yer for Johnny. Take it off. I can't."

The Old Man unstrapped the pack, and laid it before the exhausted man.

"Open it, quick."

He did so with trembling fingers. It contained only a few poor toys,—cheap and barbaric enough, goodness knows, but bright with paint and tinsel. One of them was broken; another, I fear, was irretrievably ruined by water; and on the third—ah me! there was a cruel spot.

"It don't look like much, that's a fact," said Dick ruefully ... "But it's the best we could do.... Take 'em Old Man, and put 'em in his stocking, and tell him—tell him, you know—hold me, Old Man—" The Old Man caught at his sinking figure. "Tell him," said Dick, with a weak little laugh,—"tell him Sandy Claus has come."

And even so, bedraggled, ragged, unshaven and unshorn, with one arm hanging helplessly at his side, Santa Claus came to Simpson's Bar, and fell fainting on the first threshold. The Christmas dawn came slowly after, touching the remoter peaks with the rosy warmth of ineffable love. And it looked so tenderly on Simpson's Bar that the whole mountain, as if caught in a generous action, blushed to the skies.

V
OLD CAROLS AND EXERCISES

GOD REST YOU, MERRY GENTLEMEN
OLD CAROL

God rest you, merry gentlemen,
   Let nothing you dismay,
For Jesus Christ, our Saviour,
   Was born upon this day.
To save us all from Satan's pow'r
   When we were gone astray.
O tidings of comfort and joy!
For Jesus Christ, our Saviour,
   Was born on Christmas Day.

   In Bethlehem, in Jewry,
   This blessed Babe was born.
   And laid within a manger,
   Upon this blessed morn;
The which His mother, Mary,
   Nothing did take in scorn.

From God our Heavenly Father,
   A blessed angel came;
   And unto certain shepherds
   Brought tidings of the same:
How that in Bethlehem was born
   The Son of God by name.

"Fear not," then said the angel,
   "Let nothing you affright,
   This day is born a Saviour
   Of virtue, power, and might,
So frequently to vanquish all
   The friends of Satan quite."

The shepherds at those tidings
Rejoicèd much in mind,
And left their flocks a-feeding
In tempest, storm, and wind,
And went to Bethlehem straightway,
This blessed Babe to find.

But when to Bethlehem they came,
Whereat this infant lay,
They found Him in a manger,
Where oxen feed on hay,
His mother Mary kneeling,
Unto the Lord did pray.

Now to the Lord sing praises,
All you within this place,
And with true love and brotherhood
Each other now embrace;
This holy tide of Christmas
All others doth deface.
O tidings of comfort and joy!
For Jesus Christ, our Saviour,
Was born on Christmas Day.

OLD CHRISTMAS RETURNED

All you that to feasting and mirth are inclined,
Come here is good news for to pleasure your mind,
Old Christmas is come for to keep open house,
He scorns to be guilty of starving a mouse:
Then come, boys, and welcome for diet the chief,
Plum-pudding, goose, capon, minced pies, and roast beef.

The holly and ivy about the walls wind
And show that we ought to our neighbors be kind,
Inviting each other for pastime and sport,
And where we best fare, there we most do resort;
We fail not of victuals, and that of the chief,
Plum-pudding, goose, capon, minced pies, and roast beef.

All travellers, as they do pass on their way,
At gentlemen's halls are invited to stay,
Themselves to refresh, and their horses to rest,
Since that he must be Old Christmas's guest;
Nay, the poor shall not want, but have for relief,
Plum-pudding, goose, capon, minced pies, and roast beef.

CHRISTMAS CAROL

As Joseph was a-waukin'
He heard an angel sing,
"This night shall be the birthnight
Of Christ our heavenly King.

"His birth-bed shall be neither
In housen nor in hall,
Nor in the place of paradise,
But in the oxen stall.

"He neither shall be rockèd
In silver nor in gold,
But in the wooden manger
That lieth in the mould.

"He neither shall be washen
With white wine nor with red,
But with the fair spring water
That on you shall be shed.

"He neither shall be clothèd
In purple nor in pall,
But in the fair, white linen
That usen babies all."

As Joseph was a-waukin',
Thus did the angel sing,
And Mary's son at midnight
Was born to be our King.

Then be you glad, good people,
At this time of the year;
And light you up your candles,
For His star it shineth clear.

"IN EXCELSIS GLORIA"

When Christ was born of Mary free,
In Bethlehem, in that fair citie,
Angels sang there with mirth and glee,
In Excelsis Gloria!

Herdsmen beheld these angels bright,
To them appearing with great light,
Who said, "God's Son is born this night,"
In Excelsis Gloria!

This King is come to save mankind,
As in Scripture truths we find,
Therefore this song have we in mind,
In Excelsis Gloria!

Then, dear Lord, for Thy great grace,
Grant us the bliss to see Thy face,
That we may sing to Thy solace,
In Excelsis Gloria!

THE BOAR'S HEAD CAROL
(Sung at Queen's College, Oxford.)
The boar's head in hand bear I,
Bedecked with bays and rosemary;
And I pray you, my masters, be merry,
Quot estis in convivio.
Caput apri defero
Reddens laudes domino

The boar's head, as I understand,
Is the rarest dish in all this land,
Which thus bedeck'd with a gay garland
Let us servire cantico.
Caput apri defero
Reddens laudes domino

Our steward hath provided this
In honour of the King of bliss;
Which on this day to be served is
In Reginensi Atrio.
Caput apri defero
Reddens laudes domino

CHRISTMAS CAROL

Listen, lordings, unto me, a tale I will you tell;
Which, as on this night of glee, in David's town befell.
Joseph came from Nazareth with Mary, that sweet maid;
Weary were they nigh to death, and for a lodging prayed.

In the inn they found no room; a scanty bed they made;
Soon a babe, an angel pure, was in the manger laid.
Forth He came, as light through glass, He came to save us all.
In the stable, ox and ass before their Maker fall.

Shepherds lay afield that night to keep the silly sheep,
Hosts of angels in their sight came down from Heaven's high
steep:—
Tidings! tidings unto you! to you a child is born,
Purer than the drops of dew, and brighter than the morn!

Onward then the angels sped, the shepherds onward went,—
God was in His manger bed; in worship low they bent.
In the morning see ye mind, my masters one and all,
At the altar Him to find, who lay within the stall.

Chorus.
Sing high, sing low,
Sing to and fro,
Go tell it out with speed,
Cry out and shout,
All round about,
That Christ is born indeed!
Pray whither sailed those ships all three
On Christmas day in the morning?

Oh, they sailed into Bethlehem
On Christmas day, on Christmas day;
Oh, they sailed into Bethlehem

247

On Christmas day in the morning.

And all the bells on earth shall ring
On Christmas day, on Christmas day;
And all the bells on earth shall ring
On Christmas day in the morning.

And all the angels in heaven shall sing
On Christmas day, on Christmas day;
And all the angels in heaven shall sing
On Christmas day in the morning.

And all the souls on earth shall sing
On Christmas day, on Christmas day;
And all the souls on earth shall sing
On Christmas day in the morning.

Then let us all rejoice amain
On Christmas day, on Christmas day;
Then let us all rejoice amain
On Christmas day in the morning.

A CHRISTMAS INSURRECTION
ANNE P.L. FIELD

In the hush of a shivery Christmas-tide dawn
Sing hey! sing ho! heigho!
Three small frozen figures hung stiff and forlorn
Sing hey! sing ho! heigho!
Three dim ghostly forms in the glimmering gray
Locked up in dark cold storage quarters were they
Awaiting the coming of glad Christmas day
Sing hey! sing ho! heigho!

Suspended each one from a hickory twig
Sing hey! sing ho! heigho!
A turkey, a goose, and a little fat pig
Sing hey! sing ho! heigho!
With chestnuts the turkey was garnished and stuffed
With onions and sage was the goose-carcass puffed,
While piggy was spiced, and his neck was beruffed
Sing hey! sing ho! heigho!

Three spirits regretful were hovering near
Sing hey! sing ho! heigho!
"Look!" gobbled the turkey's, "what tragedy's here!"
Sing hey! sing ho! heigho!
"For this did they tempt me with fattening food,
For this did I bring up my beautiful brood,
I always thought farmers uncommonly rude!"
Sing hey! sing ho! heigho!

The goose spirit trembled, then hissingly said
Sing hey! sing ho! heigho!
"Most men care for nothing except to be fed!"
Sing hey! sing ho! heigho!
"What horror is this, filled with onions and sage

To be served on a platter at my tender age!
'Tis enough any well-disposed fowl to enrage!"
Sing hey! sing ho! heigho!

The phantom pig grunted, "Do please look at that!"
Sing hey! sing ho! heigho!
"Oh! why did I grow up so rosy and fat!"
Sing hey! sing ho! heigho!
"They put in my mouth a sweet, juicy corncob
Just when of sensations my palate they rob,
Do you wonder such sights make a spirit-pig sob!"
Sing hey! sing ho! heigho!

Conferring, the spirits resolved on a plan
Sing hey! sing ho! heigho!
By which to wreak vengeance on merciless man
Sing hey! sing ho! heigho!
"We'll each disagree with the human inside,
We'll cause indigestion and damage his pride,
And the pains of this Christmas we'll spread far and wide!"
Sing hey! sing ho! heigho!

THE NIGHT AFTER CHRISTMAS
ANNE P.L. FIELD

Twas the night after Christmas in Santa-Claus land
And to rest from his labors St. Nicholas planned.
The reindeer were turned out to pasture and all
The ten thousand assistants discharged till the fall.
The furry great-coat was laid safely away
With the boots and the cap with its tassel so gay,
And toasting his toes by a merry wood fire,
What more could a weary old Santa desire?
So he puffed at his pipe and remarked to his wife,
"This amply makes up for my strenuous life!
From climbing down chimneys my legs fairly ache,
But it's well worth the while for the dear children's sake.
I'd bruise every bone in my body to see
The darlings' delight in a gift-laden tree!"
Just then came a sound like a telephone bell—
Though why they should have such a thing I can't tell—
St. Nick gave a snort and exclaimed in a rage,
"Bad luck to inventions of this modern age!"
He grabbed the receiver—his face wore a frown
As he roared in the mouth-piece, "I will not come down
To exchange any toys like an up-to-date store,
Ring off, I'll not listen to anything more!"
Then he settled himself by the comforting blaze
And waxed reminiscent of halcyon days
When children were happy with simplest of toys:
A doll for the girls and a drum for the boys—
But again came that noisy disturber of peace
The telephone bell—would the sound never cease?
"Run and answer it, wife, all my patience has fled,
If they keep this thing up I shall wish I were dead!
I have worked night and day the best part of a year
To supply all the children, and what do I hear—
A boy who declares he received roller-skates
When he wanted a gun—and a cross girl who states

251

That she asked for a new Victor talking machine
And I brought her a sled, so she thinks I am 'mean!'"
Poor St. Nicholas looked just the picture of woe,
He needed some auto-suggestion, you know,
To make him think things were all coming out right,
For he didn't get one wink of slumber that night!
The telephone wire was kept sizzling hot
By children disgusted with presents they'd got,
And when the bright sun showed its face in the sky
The Santa-Claus family were ready to cry!
Just then something happened—a way of escape,
Though it came in the funniest possible shape—
An aeronaut, sorely in need of a meal,
Descended for breakfast—it seemed quite ideal!
For the end of it was, he invited his host
Out to try the balloon, of whose speed he could boast.
St. Nick, who was nothing if not a good sport,
Was delighted to go, and as quick as a thought
Climbed into the car for a flight in the air—
"No telephone bells can disturb me up there!
And, wife, if it suits me I'll count it no crime
To stay up till ready for next Christmas time!"
Thus saying—he sailed in the giant balloon,
And I fear that he will not return very soon.
Now, when you ask "Central" for Santa-Claus land
She'll say, "discontinued"—and you'll understand.

WHEN THE STARS OF MORNING SANG
ANNE P.L. FIELD

When the stars of morning sang
Long ago,
Sweet the air with music rang
Through the snow,
There beside the mother mild
Slept the blessed Christmas child,—
Slumber holy, undefiled—
Here below.

When the wise men traveled far
Through the night,
Following the guiding star
Pure and bright,
Lo! it stood above the place
Sanctified by Heaven's grace,
And upon the Christ-Child's face
Shed its light.

When the world lay hushed and still
Christmas morn,
Suddenly were skies athrill—
"Christ is born!"
Angel voices, high and clear,
Chanted tidings of good cheer,
"See, the Infant King is here,
Christ is born!"

A PRAYER AT BETHLEHEM
ANNE P.L. FIELD

O pulsing earth with heart athrill
With infinite creative will!
O watchful shepherds in whose eyes
Sweet hopes and promises arise!
O angel-host whose chanting choir
Proclaims fulfillment of desire!
O flaming star so purely white
Against the black Judean night!
O blessed Mary bending low
With sense of motherhood aglow!
O holy Babe with haloed head
Soft pillowed in a manger bed!
O Mystery divine and deep
Help us Thy prophecies to keep!

THE CHRISTMAS FIRES
ANNE P.L. FIELD

The Christmas fires brightly gleam
And dance among the holly boughs,
The Christmas pudding's spicy steam
With fragrance fills the house,
While merry grows each friendly soul
Over the foaming wassail bowl.

Resplendent stands the glitt'ring tree,
Weighted with gifts for old and young,
The children's faces shine with glee,
And joyous is each tongue,
While lads and lassies come and go
Under the festive mistletoe.

When suddenly the frosty air
Is filled with music, voices sweet,
Lo! see the Christmas waits are there
Snow-crowned and bare of feet,
Yet high and clear their voices ring,
And glad their Christmas carolling.

CAROL

O Child of Mary's tender care!
O little Child so pure and fair!
Cradled within the manger hay
On that divine first Christmas day!
The hopes of every age and race
Are centered in Thy radiant face!

O Child whose glory fills the earth!
O little Child of lowly birth!
The shepherds, guided from afar,
Stood worshiping beneath the star,
And wise-men fell on bended knee
And homage offered unto Thee!

O Child of whom the angels sing!
O little Child, our Infant King!
What balm for every sorrow lies
Within those clear, illumined eyes!
O precious gift to mortals given
To win us heritage in Heaven!

THE MOTHER
ROBERT HAVEN SCHAUFFLER

All day her watch had lasted on the plateau above the town. And now the sun slanted low over the dull, blue sheen of the western sea, playing changingly with the angular mountain which rose abruptly from its surge.

The young matron did not heed the magic which was transforming the theater of hills to the north and lingering lovingly at last on the eastern summit. Nor had she any eyes for the changing hue of the ivy-clad cubes of stone that formed the village over which her hungry gaze passed, sweeping the length and breadth of the plain below.

She seemed not much above thirty: tall, erect and lithe. Her throat, bared to the breeze, was of the purest modeling; her skin of a whiteness unusual in that warm climate. Her head, a little small for her rounded figure, was crowned with a coil of chestnut hair, and her eyes glowed with a look strange to the common light of every day. It was her soul that was scanning that southward country.

From time to time she would fondle a small object hidden beneath the white folds of her robe. Once she threw her arms out in a passionate gesture toward the plain, and tears overflowed the beautiful eyes. Again she fell on her knees, and the throes of inner prayer found relief at her lips:

"Father, my Father, grant me to see him ere the dusk!"

Once again she sank down, moaning:

"He is in Thine everlasting arms. But Thou, who knowest times and seasons, give him to me on this day of days!"

Under the curve of a shielding hand her vision strained through the clear, pure air,—strained and found at last two specks far out in the plain, and followed them breathlessly as they crept nearer. One traveler was clad in a dark garment, and stopped presently, leaving his light-robed companion to hasten on alone toward the hungry-eyed woman on the plateau.

All at once she gathered her skirt with a joyous cry and ran with lithe, elastic steps down through the village.

257

They met on a low, rounded hill near the plain.

"My son, my darling!" she cried, catching him passionately to her bosom. "We have searched, and waited, and agonized," she continued after a pause, smiling at him through her happy tears.

"But it matters nothing now. I have thee again."

"My mother," said the boy as he caressed her cheek, looking at her dreamily, "I have been with my cousin. Even now he waits below for me. I must bid thee farewell. I must pass from thy face forever."

His lip trembled a little, but he smiled bravely. "For it is the will of God, the Father."

The mother's face went ashen. She tottered and would have fallen but for his slender arm about her.

Her thoughts were whirling in wild confusion, yet she knew that she must decide calmly, wisely, quickly.

Her lips moved, but made no sound.

"Oh, lay Thy wise and gracious hand upon me!" was what she breathed in silence.

Then her voice sounded rich and happy and fresh, as it had always sounded for him.

"His will be done. Thou comest to bid farewell to thy brothers and father?"

"It may not be," he answered. "My lot henceforth is to flee the touch of the world, the unsympathetic eye, the ribald tongue of those like my brothers—the defilement of common life."

The mother pressed him closer.

"Say all that is in thine heart," she murmured. "We will bide here."

They sank down together on the soft, bright turf, facing the brilliance of the west, she holding her child as of old in the hollow of her arm.

He began to speak.

"For long and long a voice within me said, 'Go and seek thy cousin.' So I sought and found, and we abode together in the woods and fields, and were friends with our dear brothers the beasts, and the fishes, and the birds. There, day by day, my

258

cousin would tell me of the dream that filled his soul and of the holy men who had put the dream there."

The mother's eyes grew larger with a swift terror, but she held her peace.

"And at the last, when the beauty, the wind, the sun, the rain, and the voice of God, had purified me in some measure, my cousin brought me to visit these holy men."

The clear, boyish voice rose and began to vibrate with enthusiasm.

"Ah, mother, *they* are the chosen ones of God! Sweet and grave and gentle they are, and theirs is the perfect life. They dwell spotless and apart from the world. They own one common purse, and spend their lives working with their hands and pondering and dreaming on purity, goodness, and the commands of the great law."

He sprang up in his excitement from her encircling arm and stood erect and wide-eyed before her.

"Ah, mother, they are so good that they would do nothing on the Sabbath, even to saving their own lives or the lives of their animals, or their brothers. They bathe very often in sacred water. They have no wives, and mortify the flesh, and—"

"What is their aim in this?" the mother interrupted gently.

The boy was aflame with his subject.

"Ah, that is it—the great goal toward which they all run," he cried. "They are doing my Father's work, and I must help! Hear, hear what is before me: When a young novice comes to them they give him the symbols of purity: a spade, an apron, and a white robe to wear at the holy meals. In a year he receives a closer fellowship and the baths of purification. After that he enters the state of bodily purity. Then little by little he enters into purity of the spirit, meekness, holiness. He becomes a temple of the Holy Spirit, and prophesies. Ah, think, mother, how sweet it would be to lie entranced there for days and weeks in an earthly paradise, with no rough world to break the spell, while the angels sing softly in one's ears! I, even I, have already tasted of that bliss."

"Say on," she breathed. "What does the holy man do then?"
"Then," the inspired, boyish tones continued—"then he performs miracles, and finally—" he clasped her hand convulsively—"he becomes Elias, the forerunner of the Messiah!"

From far out in the wilderness came a melancholy cry.

"It is John, my cousin," said the boy, radiant, half turning himself at the sound. "I must go to him."

She drew in her breath sharply, and rose to her feet.

"Bear a message to John," she said. "Not pourings of water, nor white robes; not times and seasons, nor feasts in darkness and silence, shall hasten the kingdom of heaven; neither formulas, nor phylacteries, nor madness on the Sabbath. Above all, no selfish, proud isolation shall usher in the glorious reign of the Messiah. These holy men,—these Essenes,—are but stricter, sterner, nobler Pharisees. Tell thy cousin to take all the noble and fine, to reject all the selfish and unmeaning, in their lives. Doctrine is not in heaven. Not by fasts and scourgings, not by vigils and scruples about the law; not by selfishly shutting out the world, but by taking all poor, suffering, erring, striving humanity into his heart will he become the true Elias."

There was a breathless, thrilling moment of perfect silence as the glowing eyes of the mother looked deep into the astonished, questioning eyes of the son.

Then she rested both hands on his shoulders and spoke almost in a whisper.

"As for thee, the time is now come. Does my son know what this day means?"

He looked at her wonderingly and was silent.

The mother spoke:

"For many years I have kept these things and pondered them in my heart. Now, *now* the hour is here when thou must know them."

She bent so close that a strand of loosened hair swept his forehead.

"In the time before thou wert born came as in a dream a wondrous visitor to me straight from the Father. And that pure, ecstatic messenger announced that the power of the Highest would overshadow me, and that my child was to be the son of the Highest, who should save His people from their sins—the Prince of Peace—the Messiah!"

From the wilderness came a long, melancholy cry, but the rapt boy heard not.

The mother continued in the soft, tender voice that began to tremble with her in her ecstasy.

"This day is thy birthday. Twelve years ago this eventide, when thou camest into the world of men, men came to worship and praise God for thee,—the lowliest and the highest,—as a token that thou wert to be not only Son of God but Son of Man as well. Poor, ignorant shepherds crowded about us in that little stable where we lay, and left the sweet savor of their prayers, and tears, and rejoicings. And great, wise kings from another part of the earth came also."

From beneath the folds of her robe she drew forth by a fine-spun chain an intricately chased casket of soft, yellow gold. The boy took it dreamily into his hands, and as his fingers opened it, there floated forth upon the air of the hills of Nazareth the sacred odor of incense mingled with a perfume indescribably delicate and precious.

"Read!" whispered the mother.

The boy held his breath suddenly.

There, on the lower surface of the lid, graven in rude characters, as if on the inspiration of the moment, stood the single word

LOVE

She flung wide her arms as if to embrace the universe.

"Love! Love! Love!" she cried in her rich mother's voice. "It is the greatest thing in the world! It is the message of the Messiah!"

The heavens over the sea were of molten gold, and a golden glow seemed to radiate from the boyish face that confronted them. In their trance-like ecstasy the wonderful eyes gazed full

261

into the blinding west—gazed on and on until day had passed
into night.

One iterant sound alone, as it drew closer, stirred the silence of
that evening: it was the voice of one crying in the wilderness.

THE END

www.ingramcontent.com/pod-product-compliance
Lightning Source LLC
Chambersburg PA
CBHW072358290526
45794CB00001B/106